The Witch's Yearbook

Spells, stones, tools and rituals for a year of modern magic

— Clare Gogerty —

DAVID & CHARLES

www.davidandcharles.com

Contents

A year of modern magic

Have you ever looked at a full moon on a clear winter night and shivered? Or sown a seed and marvelled as it unfurled from the earth? Have you walked in an ancient forest or sat in a stone circle and felt a deep sense of peace and belonging? Do you wonder if there is something beyond the grind of the everyday? Do you believe in magic?

If the answer to any of these questions is yes, then you need witchcraft in your life. No longer tainted by notions of sorcery, hexes and cobwebs, witchcraft has been rediscovered by those of us yearning for re-enchantment. Another way of looking at the world opens up when we take time to cast a spell, interpret the tarot, honour our ancestors with rituals or watch our pendulums swing – a new perspective filled with mystery, wonder and possibility.

This book will guide you through a year of magic. Based on the cycles of nature and guided by the seasons, it will give you the tools and know-how to unveil the magic that surrounds us. By celebrating the eight sabbats (festivals) of the Wheel of the Year, you will work with nature to activate your hidden power and trigger miraculous happenings. Witchcraft can attract love, give your career a boost, protect your home and help with healing. It will enrich your life. Whether you are a solitary hedge witch or part of a coven, a practising witch or an aspiring one, this book will take you on a year-long magical adventure.

THE WHEEL OF THE YEAR

The natural world is at the heart of witchcraft. Witches observe and respond to the seasons and cycles of nature and are guided by its wisdom. The eight chapters in this book correspond to the eight annual sabbats of the witch's calendar. These occur at equal intervals throughout the year and mark the high point of the seasons and moments in the agricultural calendar. Originally Celtic festivals, they occur at solar events called solstices and equinoxes and at the midpoints between them.

On a sabbat, witches honour gods, goddesses and nature, and are thankful for all that they provide. As well as a time of ritual and reflection, sabbats are a good opportunity to eat and drink with other witches.

Some chose to gather in covens, although many witches choose to practise alone.

The cycle of the eight sabbats is called the Wheel of the Year and is the cosmic cycle of all things: birth followed by death, then renewal. Picture the sabbats as the eight spokes on a wheel, constantly turning as surely as night follows day and summer follows winter.

Two of the eight sabbats occur at solstices (the longest and the shortest day) and two at equinoxes (when day and night are of equal length). These are the solar, or minor, sabbats, which are also known as quarter days. In the midpoints between them are the four Earth, or major, sabbats, which are also known as cross-quarter days.

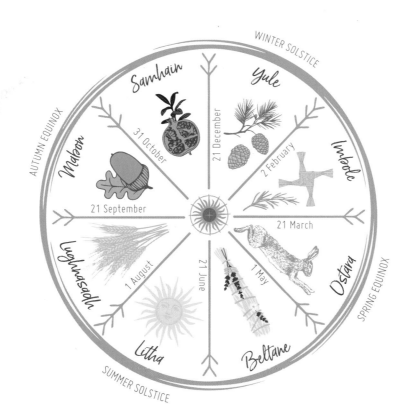

THE EIGHT SABBATS

The dates for the eight sabbats in the northern hemisphere are given below. In the Southern Hemisphere, some witches follow the traditional northern hemisphere wheel. For example, they celebrate Samhain in October. However, it can be difficult to prepare for the harvest sabbat when it is early spring. As a result, other witches work harmoniously with the cycles of nature and celebrate sabbats during the appropriate season.

SAMHAIN

IMBOLC

BELTANE

LUGHNASADH

The four major sabbats

Samhain, *31 October:* the witch's year begins. Plants die back, dead souls return. A time to prepare to descend into stillness.

Imbolc, *2 February:* the darkest days are over; the earth is preparing to burst into life.

Beltane, *1 May:* a festival of fertility. Plants sprout rapid external growth. A time of development and learning.

Lughnasadh, *1 August:* the first harvest. Plants are fruiting. A time to be grateful for what has been created.

The word 'sabbat', meaning the witch's festival, is based on a claim made by Gerald Gardner, an English witch and anthropologist. He suggested that the word was first used in the Middle Ages, and was a mixture of the Jewish Shabbat and other heretical celebrations.

The four minor sabbats:

The two solstices mark the turning points of the year.

Winter solstice (Yule), *21 December:* the shortest day. Plants are dormant. This is a time of stillness, rest and recuperation.

Summer solstice (Litha), *21 June:* the longest day. A time of intense, active energy and powerful magic.

The two equinoxes occur when the sun passes across the equator, making night and day equal across the globe.

Spring/Vernal equinox (Ostara), *21 March:* the first day of spring. Germination begins. A time of powerful energetic release.

Autumn equinox (Mabon), *21 September:* the second harvest. Seeds are dispersed. A time to take responsibility for our actions.

WORKING WITH THE FOUR ELEMENTS

The four elements of earth, air, fire and water are the basis of all life on the planet.
They are also the foundation of natural magic and central to spell work and rituals.
Each element corresponds to an astrological sign, season, colour and cardinal direction
(also called a 'quarter'). Tools used in magic work are assigned to different elements;
the governing element is used to purify the tool before magic work begins.

 Earth

Direction: north
Meaning: material abundance, fertility, work, money
Season: winter
Astrological signs: Taurus, Virgo, Capricorn
Colours: green, gold, black
Tool: the pentagram

 Fire

Direction: south
Meaning: inspiration, intuition, creativity, sexual energy
Season: summer
Astrological signs: Leo, Sagittarius, Aries
Colours: orange, red
Tool: the athame

 Air

Direction: east
Meaning: intellect, clarity of thought, communication
Season: spring
Astrological signs: Aquarius, Libra, Gemini
Colour: yellow
Tool: the wand

 Water

Direction: west
Meaning: emotions, love, psychic power
Season: Autumn
Astrological signs: Scorpio, Pisces, Cancer
Colours: blue, silver
Tool: the cauldron

The pentagram
The five-pointed star known as the pentagram is the most important symbol of witchcraft. The four lower points represent the four elements, with the uppermost point representing the fifth element: spirit. The pentagram also resembles the human form, with the head at the top and four limbs extending from the central 'body'.

Place a pentagram at the centre of your altar and have it nearby during spell work. Either draw one on a piece of paper or buy a more substantial metal or ceramic version. Before use, cleanse and charge it overnight in the light of the full moon.

When a pentagram is enclosed in a circle, it is called a pentacle. This disc is often worn by modern witches as protective jewellery and to identify themselves to other witches.

WHAT A WITCH NEEDS:

TOOLS TO MAKE YOUR MAGIC FLY

You do not need to spend a fortune to perform magic, but spell casting and rituals are much more effective with the right tools, and there are a few items that are essential. Most of these can be home-made or adapted from things you already own.

Altar

This is central to all that you do as a witch, so take a little time to set it up and decorate it. Find a place in your home where the altar will not be disturbed. This could be a mantelpiece, windowsill, shelf or a simple raised structure on a table. You do not have to buy anything special (unless you want to!); this will be your place of quiet contemplation and ritual, not a display to impress your friends. Some witches place their altars facing north – the realm of midnight, dreams and magic. Others place it facing east to honour the rising sun.

Now to decorate it... Start with your altar cloth (natural fibres like cotton or velvet work well), then add items that chime with the seasons and your intentions – you will find suggestions throughout this book. Candles, crystals and a pentacle are a good selection to start, then you can add flowers, herbs, charms – whatever feels right.

Cauldron

One of the most potent symbols of witchcraft, a cauldron, is also very handy. This round, black pot with three legs and a handle was once a common sight in homes. Hung over a fire, it was used to cook soups, broths and stews. The modern witch has a specially made cauldron, about the size of a medium saucepan, to mix herbal potions, burn incense and cast spells. It is also a lovely thing: the three legs represent the triple goddess and its full-bodied shape symbolizes Mother Earth. Cauldrons have been replaced with saucepans for cooking, and you could use one of these at a push, but they do lack magic. A cauldron is one thing worth investing in.

Athame

Pronounced a-thay-me, this is the witch's ritual knife. Never used for cutting (except for the cake at a hand-fasting ceremony), it is used to direct and control psychic energy, to draw magic circles and to call the quarters (point to the four cardinal directions) at the start of your rituals. Traditionally, an athame was made of silver or steel, with a black wooden handle. Some have double edges and are decorated with symbols and runes. It is important to treat your athame with respect. Purify and consecrate it before rituals, then wrap it in a white cloth and keep in a safe place when it is not being used.

ATHAME

CAULDRON

Book of shadows

Recording all your witchy activities in a book is a satisfying and useful thing to do. A type of supernatural journal, a book of shadows (also known as a grimoire) is an important map of your witch's journey. Use it to write up all your spells, rituals, incantations, herbal remedies and incense recipes. Do not be tempted to record all of this on a computer: it needs to be hand-written, preferably in blue ink. Keep your book of shadows safe, and remember to update it. It is an essential tool and a record of how far you have come.

Wand

Made from wood taken from a sacred tree, a wand is used to send a spell in whatever direction the wand is pointed. (To make your own, see *Witchy Craft: Make an apple wand*). Wands made from different trees have different purposes: hazel or elder make good all-round magic wands; apple wood works in love spells, and willow is good for working with lunar energies.

Crystals

These beautiful treasures from the earth will complement your magical work. Find out more about them in *Crystal Magic*.

Pentagram

This five-pointed star, the most important symbol for a witch, is a core element of witchcraft. See more about this in *Working With the Four Elements: the pentagram*.

Incense

Incense is a blend of resins, herbs, spices and oils that releases a powerful aroma when burned. It creates the right atmosphere for spell work, depending on the ingredients chosen. (To make your own, see *Winter Solstice: Make your own incense*).

Candles

The gentle light of a candle creates a calm, focused mood that will give your spells and rituals weight and potency. Lighting a candle is a sacred gesture, summoning the elements of fire and air and symbolizing the light that is born out of darkness.

It's a good idea to have a selection of candles in a variety of colours and sizes. Differently coloured candles have different meanings: pink is used for love spells, silver for clairvoyance, green to bring abundance, blue for healing and inspiration, and purple for protection. White is a neutral colour and can be used for anything. Use a fresh candle for each spell and allow it to burn down and extinguish after magic work (shorter candles or tea lights are a safer option as they burn out faster).

WAND

INCENSE ON CHARCOAL DISC

A WITCH'S HERBAL

Using plants, especially herbs, in spells and remedies is an important part of the witch's repertoire. Herbal magic is known as 'wortcunning' ('wort' means 'plant' and 'cunning' means 'knowledge') and draws on the healing and magical properties of plants.

Wise women, known as hedge or wayside witches, have always steeped leaves, pounded seeds and shredded roots and bark to use in infusions, lotions and potions. These were used for healing as well as for magic, often in recipes handed down through generations.

Plants, trees and herbs embody magical qualities that resonate at different times of the year. Those that work well with certain seasons and sabbats are recommended in the relevant chapter of this book, but do not feel restricted – work with them whenever it feels right.

Sourcing herbs

In a perfect witchy world, we would all have a herb garden lined with box hedge and labelled with each plant's name and use. (Head to a physic – medical – garden to see inspiring examples of these.) In reality, most of us are limited for space, but don't let that stop you growing herbs. A few pots on a windowsill or indoors is all it takes to have fresh spell ingredients on hand.

Alternatively, head outdoors and do a spot of foraging. Research the plant carefully beforehand, and take only what you need, never the whole plant; you will probably not need much. During the darker months, fresh plants are harder to find. Plan ahead: harvest your plants in the summer months and dry for use over winter.

Witch way: Making a herbal infusion is easy. A few sprigs infused in a pot of boiling water can work miracles. Wash 15–25g of fresh herbs in a fine strainer and add to a teapot with water from a boiling kettle. Leave to infuse for a few minutes, then it's ready to drink.
Try: mint, rosemary, lemon balm, chamomile, fennel.

HOW TO DRY FRESH HERBS

Traditionally, witches pick their herbs on a summer morning as soon as the dew has dried. This is not always practical, but do try to pick plants in their prime: you want the best specimens for drying.

Cut a few stems of your chosen herb and shake gently to remove any small insects and dirt. Wash under a running cold-water tap, then drain on a wire tray. Remove any dead or disfigured leaves and strip the lower part of the stem. Tie in bundles with string or an elastic band around the stripped part of the stem. Hang somewhere cool, dry and airy, away from direct heat or sunlight.

Every so often, rub a leaf between your finger and thumb to see if it is crisp. When it is, crumble all the leaves on to a piece of paper. Pack the crumbled herbs into an opaque jar with a sealed lid. A ceramic or dark glass jar is best to keep it fresh. Label and store in a dark, cool place.

> **A word of warning:** Some herbs are safe to use externally but can be poisonous if ingested. If the remedy is for someone else, check first for allergies.

CRYSTAL MAGIC

Stones have long been credited with magical and healing properties, especially glittering semi-precious stones that seem to radiate inner light or flash with iridescent colours.

Either quarried or appearing magically on the surface of the earth, the range and beauty of these gems is incredible and varied.

They have been used for thousands of years, their magical and spiritual power harnessed as amulets to ward off evil, to bring the wearer good luck or to cure various ailments.

The modern witch uses crystals and stones to complement their magical work, either placed on the altar, worn as jewellery, incorporated into a wand or simply carried in a pocket. Held in the hand during meditation, the right crystal will help you focus and keep you grounded.

Some witches also use crystals to heal themselves or others, either spiritually or physically. Although there is no evidence to show that crystal healing works and it is not a form of medicine, more and more people are open to trying the possible benefits that crystals bring.

It is said that you do not choose a crystal, a crystal chooses you. Every chapter of this book suggests four that are good to use during that time of year. They have been chosen to help you select the one that fits your needs; they are not prescriptive. Each stone has its own personality and energy, and how you respond to it will be different to how others do. You may find that once the crystal's work is done, you lose it or feel impelled to pass it on to someone else – and that is part of its magic.

A stone with a hole in it

The next time you go to the seaside and walk on a pebbly beach, look out for stones with holes in them. These have the unfortunate name 'hag stones', a reference to an old superstition that they kept 'hags' or witches away from your home or your animals. If hung on a stable door, your horse was safe from a witch kidnapping it and riding it to the point of exhaustion. Nowadays, these special stones are seen as a symbol of femininity and of the moon goddess Diana. Some witches collect them, and once they have 12, arrange them in a circle. Objects placed within the circle gain extra power.

CASTING A SPELL

Even with the advent of technology and advances in science, more and more of us are placing our faith in acts of magic. Belief in spells has been with us since ancient times, with methods varying according to faith system and culture. At the heart of spell making, and common to all beliefs, is a simple plea to make things better. This is communicated to a chosen deity by speech or a written note and accompanied by a ritual. Similar to prayer, a spell is a way to focus the mind, strengthen the will and ask for help. And it can be amazingly effective.

The ethics of spell working

The power of spells can be harnessed to do harm as well as good. To avoid damaging anyone or anything, it is important to have the right intention and to choose the right words before casting a spell. Follow these guidelines and you cannot go wrong:

- Never work to harm anyone.

- Never work to manipulate anyone against their will.

- Never work for your own gain at someone else's expense.

- Word your spell carefully so you do not break any of these rules.

- For extra caution, end the spell with "and may this spell work for the greatest good of all."

HOW TO CAST A SPELL

This is just one way to do spell work; there are no hard-and-fast rules. Think of it as an outline, and add extra elements and embellishments as you see fit. There are other spells throughout the book, which you can work with and adapt where necessary. Always do what feels right for you.

1. Make sure you are somewhere you are unlikely to be disturbed, then set the scene: dim the lights and burn incense that corresponds with your intention for the spell.

2. Add items to your altar that fit your mood. Light a candle or two, choosing coloured ones that complement your purpose.

3. Draw a magic circle (see *Summer Solstice: The Magic Circle*), either by walking around its circumference or drawing it in the air with your athame or wand.

4. State the purpose of your spell, either speaking it out loud, writing it on a piece of paper or both. Choose a deity or spirit guide to assist you. This could be your favourite deity or one that fits the spell, or simply put in a request to the universe.

5. Repeat your chosen incantation several times. As you say it, focus your mind and visualize the outcome. Concentrate.

6. With your wand, direct the spell out into the universe towards its goal.

7. Thank your chosen deity.

8. Unwind the circle and wait for the magic to manifest.

Take-away spells

There are times when you need a spell to take with you. Perhaps you are going on holiday and need help to make the journey go smoothly, or you want some luck for a job interview or date. Maybe a friend needs healing or assistance. The best way to take the magic with you is to make a spell pouch.

Witch way: Sprinkle some relevant herbs (you will find suggestions throughout this book) onto a square of fabric (about 10cm should do it). Add any charms and a piece of crystal. Write a few words on a piece of paper that sum up your desire and add that, too. Gather the fabric up by its corners and tie with a piece of coloured ribbon (blue for healing and protection; pink for love; green for money). Knot the ribbon five times for travel, six times for love, seven times for healing or eight times for money. If you have a little pentacle, tie that on it, too. You are ready to go!

Days to cast spells
Each day is ruled by a different planet. Choose the one that corresponds with your magic work to give your spells an extra boost.

	Planet	Star sign	Good for
Sunday	Sun	Leo	Success, career, sport, healing
Monday	Moon	Cancer	Clairvoyance, home, childbirth, women's concerns
Tuesday	Mars	Aries and Scorpio	Bravery, confrontations, men's concerns
Wednesday	Mercury	Gemini and Virgo	Communication, travel, creativity, education
Thursday	Jupiter	Sagittarius	Money, legal issues, growth
Friday	Venus	Libra and Taurus	Love, the creative arts, the environment
Saturday	Saturn	Capricorn	Property, gardening, family

MID-SEPTEMBER TO MID-NOVEMBER

Samhain
31 October

Sabbat of Samhain:
31 October*

Samhain: the witch's year begins. Plants die back, dead souls return. A time to prepare to descend into stillness.

Witchiness crackles in the air at this time of year. Stars shine brighter during the dark velvety nights and the frosty mornings twinkle with magic. The skeletal branches of trees claw at grey skies like the fingers of the crone goddess, and creatures scuttle for cover into the deepening shadows. It is the time of the third and final harvest, when the veil between this world and the next is thinnest, when the spirits of the dead slip through to join us for one night, and when plants return to the earth.

The sabbat of Samhain (pronounced *sow-en*), held on 31 October*, is the most important of the four major sabbats and is the start of the new year for witches. (The word 'samhain' translates as 'end of summer'.) On the Wheel of the Year, it is directly opposite Beltane, the spring festival of light and fertility. In contrast, Samhain is a festival of darkness and death. This descent into the stillness of deep winter is part of the cycle of life, however, and as such should be embraced. Light is born out of darkness; it is the place of new beginnings, fertile with potential.

Traditionally, as at Beltane, fires (known in Ireland as *samghnagans*) were lit on hilltops at Samhain to protect families from bad fairies. In Ireland and Scotland, home fires were extinguished to be relit from a communal bonfire. Food and drink was left out to appease the fairy folk and to ensure that livestock survived the winter. Places were set at tables for the souls of the dead, who took the opportunity of this liminal moment to revisit their old homes.

For the modern witch, Samhain is a time to remember anyone close to you who has died, and to celebrate their life. It is also a time to rest, reflect on the past year and dream and plan for the year ahead. Think of it as a time to plant seeds for your future, secure in the knowledge that they will germinate in the soft earth of your imagining and flourish in the warmer months to come.

* In the Northern Hemisphere, Samhain falls on or around 31 October. If you are in the Southern Hemisphere it will be on or around 31 April.

On your Samhain altar

Reflect this time of honouring the ancestors by adding photographs of dead family members and friends, a skull or a skeleton to your altar. Add a pumpkin or a squash, some dried leaves, a scattering of nuts and a glass of mulled wine. Black or white candles feel right, as does incense made with Dragon's blood resin powder (see Winter Solstice: *Make your own incense*).

SEEING THE FUTURE

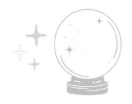

Most people are curious to know what lies ahead and want help and advice to manage it. The most valued skill that you as a witch might possess is divination – foretelling the future. With it, you can provide guidance to friends and family, and yourself, at times of change or during periods of anxiety.

Divination has been practised for centuries, whether it was the Chinese with the I Ching, the Ancient Greeks who relied on oracles, or the Ancient Egyptians and Druids who favoured scrying (see below). Nowadays, most witches have at least one tool to tune their intuition to respond to the psychic vibrations that provide clues about the future.

There are no rules or prescribed methods when it comes to divining; it depends on the individual's skill and psychic gifts. Some will find it easier than others, but everyone can improve with practice. As a witch, you must act responsibly with the information you receive. The future predicted is not fixed. It is a likely outcome that depends on circumstances at the time of the reading. Everyone has the power to shape their own future – our destinies are largely in our own hands.

Scrying

Scrying is the ancient art of looking into the future by concentrating on the shiny surface of an object until visions appear. The word 'scrying' derives from the Old English word 'descry' which means to 'make out dimly' or 'to reveal', referring to the images that appear through a thin mist. The stereotypical image of scrying is a witch with a crystal ball, but there are other, less costly ways to do it – any smooth and reflective object will work. In the past, scryers gazed into the still waters of a lake or pond at night, but most modern witches use a black mirror (see *Make a Black Mirror*). Samhain, with all its psychic potency, is a good time to scry, especially at night. Results can vary, however. Often nothing occurs at all, but at other times several visions appear either in the mirror or as mental messages. The real skill, which improves with time, is how to interpret them.

Other methods of divination

I Ching: the Chinese oracle of tossing and reading long and short yarrow sticks.

Numerology: the occult significance of numbers and their relationship to events.

Psychometry: the reading of personal objects by handling them.

Tasseomancy: the reading of tea leaves.

Palmistry: the reading of the lines of the hand.

Tarot: the reading of 78 playing cards (see *Beltane: The Tarot*)

Runes: an ancient German alphabet used for divination (see *Beltane: Runes and the Tarot*)

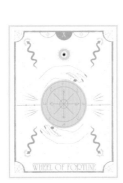

RUNE STONES

PALMISTRY

TAROT CARDS

How to scry

Choose a day that has special meaning. Samhain is ideal, or a full moon. When it gets dark, find a quiet room where you will not be disturbed. Cast your magic circle (see *Summer Solstice: The Magic Circle*) and sit inside it. Light a single candle and turn off all other lights. Burn some incense that will create the right sort of mood and help you concentrate.

Take your scrying tool, whether it's a black mirror, a crystal ball or a black cauldron filled with water. Whatever you use, it should have no flaws, bubbles or scratches. Place it on a firm surface on a black piece of cloth. Make sure the light of the candle flame does not reflect in its surface – you do not want anything distracting you.

Sit and gaze into the reflective surface. Try to keep your mind blank. This is tricky but it will become easier with practice. Try not to stare; allow your eyes to blink if they need to. Do not force something to happen by imagining anything in the reflection. Be open to what you receive.

Eventually, the scrying tool will fill with a white mist. Continue to gaze into it. In time, the mist will thin and an image will appear. This could be moving or stationary; allow whatever it is to manifest. When it vanishes, remember what you saw and consider its meaning. It could represent something that is about to occur, or it could be symbolic. It will be open to your interpretation.

After ten minutes or so, stop, whether or not you have seen something. If you did not receive an image, try again another time – it will come.

MAKE A BLACK MIRROR

Create your own scrying mirror by repurposing a piece of glass.

Witch way: Find a piece of glass of a manageable size. If you can, get an oval, concave piece, but a regular rectangular piece is perfectly good. The glass should have no imperfections or scratches in it.

Spray or paint the back of the glass with a good quality black enamel paint. Apply it as evenly as possible, and do not touch it until it is completely dry. Once dry, wrap the mirror in a piece of black velvet or similar and store safely in a box or drawer until you need it.

SAMHAIN PLANTS FOR REMEDIES AND SPELLS

Tune into the time of year with all its witchy potential by using herbs that develop your psychic powers. Use the natural power of the following four suggestions to deepen your dreams and visions.

Rosemary (*Rosmarinus officinalis*): Anyone who has grown this aromatic herb knows its familiar, pungent smell. It is one of the oldest incenses known to witches, as powerful now as ever it was. Burn it before performing magic, or wash your hands in a rosemary infusion: its sharp aroma will cleanse your magic circle and rid it of negativity. Rosemary is sacred to remembrance and is a powerful herb used for ancestor, memory or dreaming work. It also works well in a smudge stick (see *Beltane: Make a smudge stick*). Plant it in a sunny spot in well-drained soil and it will grow away happily. It is also known as Elf Leaf: reason enough to include it in your witch's herb garden!

Wormwood (*Artemisia absinthium*): A bitter and potent herb, wormwood is one of the ingredients of the dangerously alcoholic drink absinthe (the others are fennel and anise), also known as the Green Witch. Best to avoid the ruinous effects of this poky drink and stick to using wormwood in incense (good for developing psychic powers) or drying it and burning in your cauldron to summon spirits. According to old grimoires, if it is burned in a graveyard, the spirits of the dead will rise. It has also been credited as an antidote to the effects of toadstools and hemlock or a bite from a sea dragon, but modern medicine is a better alternative. You could hang wormwood from a rear-view mirror in your car – it is supposed to protect you on dangerous roads.

Mugwort (*Artemisia vulgaris*): Blooming from June to September with clusters of white/green flowers on tall stems, mugwort is a visionary herb, used in witchcraft to boost divinatory powers. It appears in ancient recipes for flying ointments, psychic teas and divinatory incense. Dried mugwort was one of the nine sacred herbs of the Anglo Saxons*, and was burned in rituals and ceremonies. A Medieval ale called 'gruit' was brewed with mugwort, myrtle and yarrow and served in large mugs, which is said to be how the herb got its name. The modern witch might like to harness this herb's divinatory powers to cleanse a crystal ball or other scrying tools, or include it in a spell pouch or visionary tea. You could also put some in your shoes – it is said to pep you up if you are feeling weary.

* Seven of the others are watercress, camomile, nettle, apple, chervil, plantain and fennel. The ninth remains a mystery but could possibly be betony or hairy bittercress.

Persephone and the pomegranate

Let Greek mythology be your guide, and include a pomegranate or its seeds in your spell work at Samhain. This peculiar fruit, with its leathery casing and masses of juicy crimson seeds (called arils) enclosed in a web of white chambers, is not just great for sprinkling on salads; it is a symbol of the underworld, fertility and good luck.

The story goes that Demeter, goddess of the harvest and fertility, had a much-loved and over-protected daughter called Persephone. The god of the underworld, Hades, a frustrated suitor, rose from the ground in his chariot and snatched her. A heart-broken Demeter wandered the earth looking for her lost daughter. While she did so, the harvest perished. When Persephone was eventually located, an agreement was made between her mother and Hades, now Persephone's husband, that she would spend half of the year above ground (spring and summer) and the other half in the underworld (autumn and winter). Persephone had eaten six of twelve pomegranate seeds when she first went to the underworld, and this number governed how many months she would spend above and beneath the ground each year.

Blessed Thistle (*Cnicus benedictus*): This tough and spiky thistle thrives where little else flourishes, keeping animal and human marauders at bay. Use its prickly quality in charms and rituals to protect yourself and your home and to ward off negativity. In the Middle Ages it was regarded as a healing herb, especially for liver complaints. Drunk as an infusion or burned in incense, it can also clear the mind, allowing creativity and inspiration space to shine.

Witch ways: Here are some ways you can reap the benefits of these seasonal plants. See *A Witch's Herbal* for directions on making infusions and drying herbs.

- Make an infusion with rosemary, lavender and mugwort, add a spoonful of honey and invite your ancestors to join you for tea.

- Make a mugwort infusion and use sparingly to deter insects by spritzing onto plants with a mister, or dry its leaves and hang in the wardrobe to keep moths at bay.

- Include some wormwood in an incense mix to develop your psychic powers (see *Winter Solstice: Make your own incense*).

- From Cunninghams's *Encylopedia of Magical Herbs*: 'Place some thistle in boiling water. Remove from heat and lie or sit beside it. As the steam rises, call the spirits and listen carefully; they may answer your questions.'

BLESSED THISTLE

CRYSTALS FOR SAMHAIN

Choose a magical stone to help you make contact with your ancestors. This is a good time to meditate with a crystal that will cultivate your wisdom and presence. These feel powerful now:

Black Obsidian: mysterious glassy stone formed by fire. Formed at the end of a volcanic eruption, obsidian is lava hardened into a glossy black rock. Without imperfections, it is ideal to use for a scrying mirror or crystal ball, and has been favoured by occultists and shaman for centuries. Gaze into its fathomless depths and you could face your true self – one of the reasons the stone is called the Warrior of Truth. It is also said that obsidian's protective shield enables safe past life and ancestral work. This stone can be carved easily: arrowheads, knives and axe heads have been fashioned from it since the Stone Age. The pupils of the eyes of the Moai statues on Easter Island are made from obsidian.

Fluorite: clusters of visionary crystals.
Luminous and glassy, fluorite forms in clusters of columns and cubes that stand proud from the rock that contains it. It ranges in colour from purple to green, yellow and blue, each often occurring as stripes in one block. Known as the Genius Stone, it can help you work through complex problems and amplifies creativity. Fluorite has long been associated with mysticism, psychic awareness and intuition. Used in meditation, it can produce rich visions and insights.

Labradorite: a shard of iridescent brilliance.
Associated with divination and intuition, this is a good stone for Samhain magic. According to the Inuit people of North America, it fell down from the frozen fire of the Aurora Borealis. Its incredible shimmering colour with iridescent flashes of peacock blue, gold, pale green and coppery red is like a shard of that natural phenomenon and gives the stone a rare, magical quality. Originally discovered by Moravian missionaries in Labrador, Canada (hence its name), it is a Stone of Magic, used by shaman, diviners and anyone seeking knowledge and guidance.

Labradorite is also said to enhance clairvoyance and assist communication with spirits.

Black tourmaline: deep, dark and opaque.
It is said that ancient magicians used this black crystal to protect themselves from demons. It is still used as a psychic shield during ritual work: place eight small tumbled stones in a circle on your altar to keep you safe. Black or very deep blue, it forms in vertical structures, and may be transparent or opaque. Polished, the opaque form can be used for scrying. Try rubbing or heating it gently: it will become electrically charged.

DESIGN A CRYSTAL GRID

Place crystals on a grid-like pattern to amplify their power and manifest your dreams and intentions.

A spiral, heart or wheel are simple shapes to start with, but your grid can be as elaborate as you like. Some witches place their crystals on complex mandalas, designs based on sacred geometry or patterns created by nature. You will need at least four crystals. Charge them in the sun or beneath a full moon, then focus on your intention as you place the largest stone in the centre of your grid and lay the others around it, following the pattern.

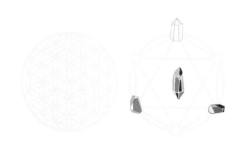

SAMHAIN TRADITIONS AND CUSTOMS

For most people, 31 October is known as Halloween, when gaggles of children in ghoulish garb go trick or treating, shops are filled with chocolate ghosts, and pumpkins are carved into fiendish forms. Halloween, however, is the Christianized version of Samhain. For Christians it is the eve of All Hallows Day, when the dead – including saints and martyrs – are remembered.

Jack-o-lanterns

Carving pumpkins for Halloween originated in the Middle Ages when turnips or mangelwurzels (a beet vegetable grown as livestock fodder) were hollowed out, carved into grotesque faces, filled with coals, lit, then hung from strings on sticks. These jack-o-lanterns represented the spirits of supernatural beings and were used to ward off any evil spirits out and about that night. On Punkie Night, the last Thursday in October, they were carried around villages in Ireland, Scotland and Somerset by children. ('Punkie' is an old name for a lantern.) Led by the Punkie King and Queen, the children marched and sang this song:

It's Punkie Night tonight

It's Punkie Night tonight

Adam and Eve would not believe

It's Punkie Night tonight

Give me a candle give me light If you haven't a candle, a penny's all right

The demand for a candle, which included a threat if one was not forthcoming, is thought to be the origins of trick or treating. Punkie Night has been revived in some Somerset villages, including Hinton St. George where it is a popular annual festival.

Apple dunking

If you have ever found yourself on Samhain upside down in a bowl of water, hands tied behind your back, trying to get your teeth around a bobbing apple, you will know the perils of apple dunking. Also called apple bobbing, nowadays it is played as a game with the person nabbing the most apples being proclaimed the winner. Originally, however, it had a divinatory purpose: it would reveal the name of your true love.

This is how it worked: once an apple had been secured in the teeth, it was peeled carefully to keep the peel in once piece. This was then passed *deosil* (clockwise) around the head before being tossed over the shoulder to the ground. The peel would fall into a shape resembling an initial letter: that of your future spouse.

Another divination game was to string apples from the ceiling, then bite and peel them, casting the peel onto the floor as in apple dunking. Shells of nuts were also thrown into the fire. If the nuts burned slowly, true love was coming. If they popped and cracked and were spat out by the fire, you could expect a mere infatuation.

SAMHAIN RITUALS AND SPELLS

For some witches, this is the most powerful time of the year for magic work, especially if it involves contacting the spirit world. It is when the veil between this world and the next is thinnest, so dead souls can slip back and join us.

Solo ritual

This is a good time to remember family members, friends and pets who have died. Find photographs and mementos associated with them and display them on your altar or on a sideboard or table. Surround them with tea lights or votive candles (a candle that is slightly larger than a tea light, often made of beeswax and intended to be burned as an act of prayer). As you light the candles, speak the names of the dead. Thank them for being part of your life and for what they brought to it. Sit quietly and notice any messages you receive.

A SIMPLE SAMHAIN SPELL
TO MAKE CHANGE HAPPEN

The witch's new year is the time to plan that thing you have always wanted to do. Whether it is changing jobs, moving home, travelling or something else, now is the moment to cast a spell to help make that leap.

WHAT YOU NEED

- 2 blue candles
- crystals or stones of your choosing
- incense of your choosing
- a piece of paper and a pen

On a Monday night during the waxing moon (see: *Winter Solstice: The Moon*), light both candles, place them on your altar and surround them with crystals. Light the incense (see *Winter Solstice: Make your own incense*). On the paper, write down what you want to change. Offer the paper to the candle, and, as it burns, say the following incantation five times:

Goddess and the universe
Listen now to me
Help me make the changes I can see
So I might at last be who I want to be
So mote it be

Let the candles burn out. Repeat the same spell for the next five nights with a single candle. Allow it to burn down completely.

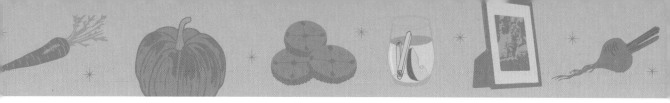

A Samhain ritual with your witchy crew: throw a Dumb Supper

This is a simple and effective way to remember dead loved ones and to help with grief. It works especially well when everyone knew the person who has died, whether you are a group of friends or members of a family.

Prepare a Samhain feast, aiming to include seasonal ingredients like pumpkins or squash, root vegetables and mulled cider. You could also cook Soul Cakes, a traditional English biscuit made with currants at this time of year.

Light a candle in the window to guide your guests and the dead to the table.

Set the table and include one extra place for the dead person. Place a candle in the centre of the table and a tea light or a votive candle at each person's place.

When everyone arrives, switch off the lights and sit in darkness. Say: "As we celebrate Samhain, we invite our departed loved ones to join us in this home."

Light the central candle and everyone says: "Welcome [name of departed person or people] we honour your presence among us."

Say a few words about what you remember about that person, then light your tealight from the central candle. Working around the table, everyone else does the same.

You say: "We thank you for coming to join us at our Samhain feast. We also thank the earth for all it has given us this season, the fruits of which we will enjoy this evening. We are grateful for the summer's harvest and look forward to winter, a time of sacred darkness and becoming. So mote it be."

Everyone says: "So mote it be."

Allow the candles to die out as you eat and drink, celebrating the life of the deceased and the blessings of the time of year.

WITCHY CRAFT

MAKE A NEW YEAR SPELL JAR

Samhain is the time to reflect on the past year — its excitements and its disappointments — and make plans for the next. Putting your intentions on paper and then into a spell jar alongside other magical elements is a good way to make them happen. The best time to do this is at a full moon, when lunar energy is most powerful.

Prepare your container: let your intuition and your intentions guide you when you choose what to put in your jar. First, add the sea salt or sand to hold the tea light steady. Sit the tea light on top – this is your anchor. Now surround this with your other ingredients. There is no strict recipe: what you include is up to you. Here are some suggestions.

Pound some dried herbs and spices into dust in a mortar and pestle – you could try one or two of the following: basil for wealth; lavender for peace; holly for protection; cinnamon for love; cloves for good luck; sage for wisdom. You could also add talismans that connect powerfully with you, like a pebble picked up from a beach, pressed petals from a flower given to you by a loved one, a coin or a small charm. Perhaps add a strand or two of you own hair, nail clippings, blood or saliva to connect yourself strongly with the spell. Include eggshells to give you strength to start something new.

Write your intention for the year ahead on a piece of paper and drop that in, too.

WHAT YOU NEED

- a small, wide glass jar with a lid – it should have enough room for a tea light and all the other elements you include in your spell

- a tea light, plus sea salt or sand to keep it steady

- dried herbs and spices (see suggestions, left)

- talismans (see suggestions, left)

- string and wax to seal the jar

Activate your spell jar

Follow these steps to make the magic happen.

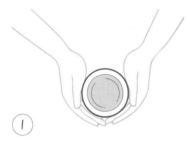

1 Hold the jar and think about your intention and your hopes for the year ahead.

TEA LIGHT

2 Put each item into the jar carefully, starting with the sand, then the tea light, then packing the rest around it. As you do so, think about why you chose each thing and how it will help you.

3 Place the jar in moonlight (at the full moon is best) for an hour or so to charge it.

4 Light the tea light and ask your goddess or the universe for help to make your year a success. Put the lid on the jar, extinguishing the flame.

5 Tie the string around the lid. To seal the jar with wax, heat the end of the wax stick over a tea light or lighter, then carefully let the hot wax drip onto the string.

6 Place the jar in an appropriate place: on your altar so you can recharge it and use it for meditation practice; in the garden to encourage personal growth; or by your bedside to remind you of your intention.

> **A word of warning:** Care is needed when sealing the jar, as molten wax can burn.

Yule

21 December

Sabbat of the Winter Solstice: 21 December*

Winter solstice: the shortest day. Plants are dormant. This is a time of stillness, rest and recuperation.

Magic shivers in the air at midwinter. Bare branches of trees outlined against pale wintry skies are skeletal and boughed with snow. Migratory birds that filled the summer air with song have flown. Crisp mornings twinkle with frost, slowly melting as the days slip into darkness. On a clear night, the three bright stars of Orion's belt shine brightly, and the full moon is ringed by a winter halo of ice crystals. Shadows are darker now, the ground is harder, and creatures slumber. It is a still, silent time of mystery and bewitchment.

At the heart of midwinter is the winter solstice*, the turning point of the year, when the earth is poised to change. This is the shortest day of the year, when the sun reaches a point directly above the Tropic of Capricorn and seems to hang still in the sky. ('Solstice' is from the Latin *sol* – sun, and *sistere* – to stand still). The following morning, though, life begins again as the days lengthen and the light starts to return, bringing hope and the promise of renewal.

The modern witch, always sensitive to the changes of the season and the power inherent in each, adapts her rituals and spells accordingly. Midwinter is a time to celebrate the imminent return of the light with family and friends, but it is also a time to start again. It is an opportunity to step aside from normal life and 'mini-hibernate'. Quiet reflection and meditation alongside rituals and spell-casting provide a chance to think about the year that has passed and to shape the year to come.

* In the Northern Hemisphere, the winter solstice falls on or around 21 December. If you are in the Southern Hemisphere, i.e. below the equator, it will be on or around 21 June.

On your winter solstice altar

This is the time to really make your altar sparkle and shine. Begin with tangles of evergreen foliage like mistletoe, ivy and holly. Place red and white candles among it in glittering gold holders to symbolize the return of the sun and light banishing darkness. Add a piece of ice-white quartz to bring healing, and add pine cones – a symbol of potential fertility, and a reminder of the burst of life to come in spring.

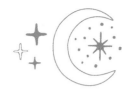

THE MOON

On a clear night, nothing is as magical as the full moon rising into the sky, casting its silvery light on the Earth, transforming the darkness into something unworldly. The moon is the ruler of the night, a thing of majesty and wonder. It has always inspired awe – primitive people believed it to be the source of all fertility. Because its phases correspond with the monthly cycle of women, this association with fertility and feminine power continues. The moon also controls the tides, and as the sea is a powerful symbol of the subconscious, it governs intuition, psychic ability and dreams.

The modern witch harnesses the magic and mysteries of the ever-changing moon in all her magical activities. Some see it as the actual source of their power, with high priestesses in covens 'drawing' its goddess spirit down from the sky to enter them and perform magic.

For all witches, whether in a coven or practising alone, an awareness of the lunar cycle and its varying energies is essential for the practice of their craft.

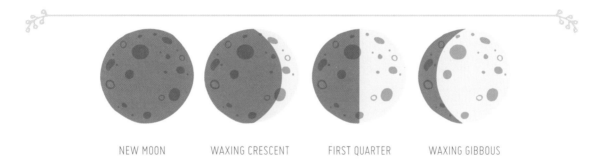

NEW MOON   WAXING CRESCENT   FIRST QUARTER   WAXING GIBBOUS

The phases of the moon

The moon is very bright but it does not shine from within – it reflects the sun. As the moon orbits the Earth and the Earth orbits the sun, the lunar phases gradually change as reflected sunlight falls on different parts of its surface. Each lunar phase has its own type of energy. Working harmoniously with each will power your spells.

New moon: the moon appears to vanish as reflected sunlight hits its far side and the shadow of the Earth entirely covers it.
Working with the moon's energies: this is a time to cast spells to help new projects flourish and is also the moment to plant seeds. The moon is technically only

new for a moment, when the sun and moon directly align, although its energy lasts for three days. Some witches avoid casting spells in the three days prior to the new moon, although others thought it an especially potent time. The day of the new moon can be a time to initiate new members into the coven.

Waxing moon: the bright crescent appears on the right-hand side of the moon and increases (waxes) until it becomes a full moon.
Working with the moon's energies: As the moon appears to grow larger, continue to sow seeds and put your plans into action. This is a time of growth.

FULL MOON	WANING GIBBOUS	LAST QUARTER	WANING CRESCENT

Full moon: the moon is fully illuminated. This circle of mottled brightness – sometimes silver, sometimes golden – casts a pale white light over the world below. On rare occasions there are 13 full moons in a year, with a single month including two full moons. The rare second full moon is called a blue moon. This can occur at different times of the year.

Working with the moon's energies: The moon's energies are particularly potent now. This is a magical time when most covens meet, when spells are most powerful and when plans begin to manifest.

Waning moon: the bright crescent appears on the left-hand side of the moon and decreases until it vanishes at the new moon.

Working with the moon's energies: This is a time of diminishing and destruction. Let go of what is not working to make room for what does. Spells that help break bad habits or addictions are effective now.

Moon bathing

Unlike sunbathing, lying in the light of the moon does not damage your skin or create wrinkles. Instead it recharges the spirit, refreshes the body and boosts psychic powers. It is also a simple meditative experience that calms the mind and steadies the nerves.

Witch way: lie in a place where the moon bathes your entire body. You could do this naked ('skyclad') or in your pyjamas: either works! Remember the moon moves across the sky during the night, so you may have to shift your position for a lunar top-up. Moons at different times of the year look different and will have different effects. The winter moon is silvery, silent and calming; the spring moon has a rejuvenating green tinge; the summer moon casts a yellowish light that boosts energy levels; and the mellow autumn moon brings serenity.

MAKE MOON WATER

Charge a glass of water with lunar energy to use in spells or bless crystals.

Witch way: Fill a glass or jar with water (rainwater or spring water is best, but filtered tap water will do). You could also sprinkle in a pinch of sea salt and drop in a clear quartz crystal for extra whizz. Hold the glass close to your heart and visualize it filling with light and love, then place it in the light of the full moon. Surround it with talismans, herbs and crystals that chime with a particular intention or wish, then leave until morning. Use the charged water to power up crystals and increase their potency, add a splash to your bath, use it to wash your hair (said to improve mental clarity) or spritz it around the house as a blessing.

A simple new moon ritual

The evening of a new moon is a good time to take stock of your life. The energy of the moon will help you to reflect and set new intentions.

Witch way: Find a quiet place where you are unlikely to be disturbed, either in the house or outside. Create a cleansing atmosphere by burning incense that includes rosemary or mugwort, or add some essential oils to a diffuser. Sit quietly with your eyes shut and picture the moon growing through the month. Think of the ways you would also like to grow. When you have come up with a direction, gently open your eyes and write down your thoughts.

WINTER PLANTS FOR REMEDIES AND SPELLS

During this time when flowering plants die back and many trees are bare, plants that carry berries or keep their leaves are especially valued by the hedge witch. Four in particular are endowed with potency and magic and can be used in remedies, teas, spells and ceremonies.

Mistletoe *(Viscum album):* The pure white berries and evergreen leaves of mistletoe stand out in the depths of winter when trees are bare. The way it grows is particularly intriguing: its seeds, dropped by birds, germinate and grow on the boughs of trees. This apparent ability to grow from nothing, suspended far from the earth, is a wonderful and mysterious thing, especially if the tree is a sacred oak or apple. It was once believed that mistletoe absorbed the magical properties of its host tree and had to be cut at the winter solstice with a silver knife.

Holly *(Ilex):* The leaves of this tree with their spiky bristles are used to repel unwanted spirits and for general protection. Its bright, glossy red berries – so cheery when all around is muted and grey – symbolize feminine blood and represent the miracle of birth. In folklore, the Holly King is the personification of the dark half of the wheel of the year (the Oak King represents the light half) and is at the height of his power in midwinter. Some believe he is a precursor of Santa Claus.

Ivy *(Hedera):* Sinuous, tough and evergreen, the ivy grows in a spiral around its host plant, often continuing to grow after the host has died. It was believed to heal sick animals, especially cattle, and some farmers fed a piece of ivy to each animal before noon on Christmas Day to keep the Devil away for a year. It symbolizes immortality and resurrection and can be used in magic for healing and to bind lovers tightly together.

> **A word of warning:** Mistletoe is poisonous so hang it out of reach around the home, or add the berries to a spell pouch, but do not ingest as a potion or a tea

Winter solstice celebrations around the world

Dongzhi ('arrival of winter'), *China, 21 – 23 December.* Families get together to celebrate the passing year with special food like *tangyuan* (glutinous rice balls), which symbolise reunion.

St. Lucia's Day, *Scandinavia, 21 – 22 December.* Fires are lit to ward off spirits during the longest nights of winter. Girls dress in white gowns with red sashes and candle crowns in honour of the Christian martyr, St. Lucia.

Yaldá, *Iran, 21 December.* Red fruit such as pomegranates and watermelons are eaten to symbolize the crimson dawn, as people gather to feast and read poetry.

Soyal, *northern Arizona, 21 December.* Hopi Indians perform purification rituals and ceremonies and welcome the *kachinas* (protective spirits) from the mountains.

Yew *(Taxus baccata):* This most venerable tree lives for centuries, often decaying from the inside out, leaving a hollow big enough to stand inside. Evergreen, with poisonous red cup-shaped berries that enclose a poisonous seed, it has long been held sacred and is used to contact the ancestors or to reach the underworld. It was also the sacred tree of Hecate, a Greek goddess (see *Imbolc: The Goddess*), when she appears in her guise as a wise crone in the dark half of the year. Wands made of yew are thought to be especially powerful when working with the ancestors or used in spells around longevity.

Witch ways: Here are a few ways that you can harness the seasonal power of these midwinter plants.

• Sprinkle new-born babies with 'holly water' (water steeped with holly overnight) to bless them and bring them good fortune.

• Hang a sprig of holly over your front door or weave among other evergreens into a wreath: its prickly leaves will protect your home and its occupants, and the wreath will represent the wheel of the year.

• Hang a bough of mistletoe in the house to protect against fire, illness and bad luck.

• Suspend mistletoe from the ceiling and invite a favoured person (or two!) to kiss you. After each kiss, remove a berry until none remain. This popular yuletide custom is said to have originated as a Druidic fertility rite.

YEW

A word of warning: It is best to buy a ready-made yew wand rather than whittle your own, as even shavings of yew wood can be deadly.

CRYSTALS FOR THE WINTER SOLSTICE

During the short, dark days of winter, bring the power of
the sun and the energy of fire into your witchy practice
with crystals. These feel powerful now:

Garnet: a deep red stone with fire at its heart.
Dark red garnet is perfect for winter solstice rituals.
It adorned Egyptian burial jewellery, was popular in
Ancient Rome and still is with Native American people.
Symbolizing the vitality and strength of fire, it is known
as the Warrior's Stone. It energizes, strengthens and
protects. As a talisman, it will help you create the life you
desire in the year ahead. It is the birthstone for January
and is associated with the root chakra (see box).

Bloodstone (heliotrope): flecked with jasper.
Earthy green with flecks of blood-red jasper, this is a
powerful healing stone. It has been used for centuries,
including by Classical magicians who believed it made
them invisible, and by the Gnostics who wore it as an
amulet to lengthen their lives and strengthen their
courage. At this time of year, it can be used in spells to
boost flagging energy, confidence or bravery.

Ruby: precious and fiery, perfect for the solstice.
Red ruby is one of the five traditional cardinal gems.
The others are amethyst (purple), diamond (white),
emerald (green) and sapphire (blue). If you are lucky
enough to own one, this fiery and powerful crystal will
be particularly effective when used as part of your winter
solstice rituals, especially to help manifest intentions for
the year ahead.

Carnelian: a translucent chunk of glowing red.
This is another fiery red stone, although the colour can
vary from pale orange to almost black. It symbolizes
fertility and abundance, so fits nicely with the mood of
this season, which is all about new ideas, new beginnings
and new life. Carnelian is often made into jewellery, and
wearing it in a bracelet or ring heightens creativity –
handy if you are stuck on a project or about to start a
new one.

Crystals and chakras: a basic guide

'Chakra' is a Sanskrit word meaning 'wheel' and
refers to the seven spheres of energy that run
up the spine. Although not a witchcraft practice,
working on the body's chakra system can be
powerful, especially when combined with crystals.
Here's an outline:

The seven major chakras

1. **Root chakra** at the base of the spine.

Colours: red or black.
Crystals: garnet, ruby, black tourmaline.

2. **Sacral chakra** in the lower abdomen.

Colour: orange.
Crystals: carnelian, citrine, moonstone, opal.

3. **Solar plexus chakra** in the upper abdomen.

Colour: yellow.
Crystals: jasper, amber, golden topaz.

4. **Heart chakra** just above the heart.

Colours: green or pink.
Crystals: rose quartz, peridot, aventurine.

5. **Throat chakra** at the throat.

Colour: blue.
Crystals: turquoise, lapis lazuli, aquamarine.

6. **Third Eye chakra** at the forehead.

Colour: indigo.
Crystals: amethyst, purple fluorite.

7. **Crown chakra** at the top of the head.

Colours: violet or white.
Crystals: labradorite, clear quartz.

WINTER SOLSTICE TRADITIONS AND CUSTOMS

Bringing evergreen foliage into the house is an old custom that is more than merely decorative. Boughs of holly, ivy and mistletoe twined into wreaths connect us with the natural world that is sleeping outside the window, reminding us that spring is on its way.

The Yule* log

One folklore tradition, dating from pre-Christian times, brings an entire tree trunk into the house. This may have Druidic origins: they venerated trees, and the oak in particular. Bringing a piece of oak indoors brought the Oak God with it and guaranteed the return of spring. A log was cut down or given as a gift; if it was bought or sold, its magical properties were destroyed. It was decorated with evergreen foliage and dragged into the hearth, sprinkled with cider or ale and set alight. The challenge was to keep it burning steadily until Twelfth Night (6 January or old Twelfth Night on 17 January): if the fire went out before then, bad luck would follow. A piece of unburnt wood was kept to light the following year's log.

Witch way: Dragging a tree trunk into the house is out of the question for most modern witches. Instead, make a mini Yule log from a 25cm long branch (preferably oak). Drill three holes into the branch. Wrap silver foil around the base of three red candles and put them in the holes. Decorate with holly, ivy and mistletoe. Light the candles and leave to burn until Twelfth Night.

* Yule, an old German word for the Christmas festival, was dedicated to the god Odin. Many witches have adopted its name to use for the winter solstice.

Wassailing

In the UK, the custom of 'wassailing' the oldest apple tree in the orchard on Twelfth Night is making a comeback. Increasing numbers of people are gathering in orchards, where they drink mulled cider from a wassail bowl and sing traditional songs. A piece of toast soaked in cider (known as the Apple Tree Man) is placed in the branches of the oldest tree for the robins, who embody the spirit of the apple trees. This is to ward off evil spirits and ask the trees to produce a fine harvest of apples the next year. The last apple is often left on the tree at harvest time for the Apple Tree Man to ensure a good crop.

The Yule candle

A candle kept alive through the darkest days is a symbol of light and a reminder that it will return. A large candle is needed so it will keep burning – green or red is traditional for midwinter. Several traditions surround the Yule candle: it should only be extinguished with a snuffer – blowing it out brings bad luck – and the only person who can do this is the head of the household. Any part of the candle that remains after Twelfth Night can be set aside to light during a thunderstorm – it is said to prevent lightning strikes. The Yule candle is placed in a window for passersby to see and to spread goodwill and seasonal cheer.

YULE CANDLE

YULE LOG

WASSAIL BOWL

WINTER SOLSTICE RITUALS AND SPELLS

Try to find a moment or two to step away from all the commotion and carry-on at Christmas. It is important to sit quietly and settle into and respond to the time of year.

Simple solo sunrise ritual

On the morning of the winter solstice, go for a solitary walk to somewhere you can watch the sun rise. Stepping away from your normal environment and setting off on a mini-adventure brings its own magic. Find a place that has a good view of the rising sun: a hill is best, but a tall building or even your back garden or balcony could also work if going further is tricky. As you wait for the sun to come up, write a list of wishes for friends and family on a piece of paper. Fold it up and take it home to put on your altar with anything else you may have found on your journey, to remind you of the moment and your intentions and wishes.

WINTER SOLSTICE SPELL

WHAT YOU NEED

- a red candle
- a circle of paper
- mistletoe berries
- a red pen
- your cauldron or a saucepan

Think of a word that represents your hopes for the year ahead. This could be 'love' if that is what you want to attract, or 'money', or anything else at all. On a circle of paper, about 5cm in diameter, write that word in red. Drop a couple of mistletoe berries onto the middle of the circle. Add a sprinkling of herbs that have meaning to you. Twist the paper so that the berries are enclosed. Light a red candle and carefully burn the paper and its contents over the cauldron or saucepan. As it burns, visualize your word becoming a reality. When it has burned (mind your fingers!), let the ashes drop into the cauldron or pan, blow out the candle and sit quietly as the spell disperses its magic into the world around you.

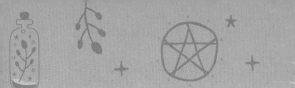

A winter solstice ritual with your witchy crew

First, cast your circle (see *Summer Solstice: Casting a circle*). Then, light a red candle and place it on your altar in the centre of the circle. Gather your friends and stand at an evenly spaced distance around it. Each person places a smaller candle – a tea light works well – at their feet. Turn off the lights so that it is as dark as you can make it.

Recite the following words, asking your friends to respond as indicated.

You say: "Welcome everyone. Let us celebrate being here to honour the winter solstice and the turning of the year."

Everyone says: "We are grateful for the peace of the darkness."

You say: "We shall now make the call for peace."

You say: "Let us welcome the darkness of this the longest night, and honour its power to transform and teach. From this point of greatest darkness comes the beginning of the light. What new hopes and dreams are waiting to grow?"

Going around the circle, each person says aloud their hopes and dreams as they light their own candle from the central flame.

You say: "As the darkness ends, let us let go of everything that has held us back this year. What will you cast away into the dying darkness?"

Everyone blows their candle out, then stays still and mentally releases any pain, anxieties or disappointments they experienced over the previous year.

You say: "As the fears of last year vanish into the night, we welcome back the life-giving light of the sun. Let the hopes and dreams of the new year flourish in its warmth."

Everyone says: "We believe in our magic and its power to manifest our wishes."

You say: "So it is. So it shall be done. It is done!"

Everyone says: "So mote it be."

The lights are turned back on and the ritual is over. Feasting begins!

WITCHY CRAFT

MAKE YOUR OWN INCENSE

Scented smoke creates a wonderful atmosphere for magic, wreathing you and your cauldron in its aromatic embrace. Making and lighting incense is spell-binding in itself, and it is a central component in a witch's work. The power of aromatic herbs, spices, oils, resins and bark has an ancient history, long used as a ritual tool to create a sacred space. Incense has the power to inspire a magical state of mind and fill your house with sublime fragrance.

How to use incense

Traditionally, especially in Roman Catholic churches, incense is burned in a censer (also known as a thurible), a perforated metal container that is swung on a chain so the scented smoke envelops the congregation. Most of us, however, do not have a censer (or the room to swing one!), so burning incense on a charcoal disc or in your metal cauldron is the best option. You can also buy ready-made incense or use incense sticks or cones, which are easier to manage but less fun. Essential oils released in an infuser are a good option for those who do not like smoke.

To make your own incense, customize the ingredients listed to suit your purpose or taste. The following suggestions can be used alone or in combination or substituted with your favourites – experiment to see what works best for you. They can all be bought online.

Amber: a blend of musk and floral resins, this complex incense can be used on its own or blended with others. It brings wisdom and truth.

Dragon's Blood: the authentic tree resin is rare and expensive, but a good quality synthetic powdered resin is neither, and makes a good substitute. It will add a fiery energy to love magic and boosts most others.

Frankincense: this ancient and holy tree resin is good for cleansing a space, consecrating your tools and spell work.

Myrrh: Often used with frankincense, this ancient tree resin is good for ancestor work and banishing negativity.

Lavender: the soothing aroma of lavender is helpful during meditation and healing work.

Pine: the resin from coniferous trees smells like a woodland floor. It will lend wisdom and protection to your magic work and is good for money spells.

WHAT YOU NEED

- 25g frankincense resin
- 3 pinches of Dragon's Blood resin powder
- 10g pine resin
- 15g myrrh resin and a small handful of calendula (or choose from the list of incense ingredients above)
- a charcoal disc
- an incense burner

Concoct a fragrant potion

Follow these steps to make your incense. Think about why you are making the incense: your intention. Are you hoping for a vision or a dream? Do you want to make contact with the dead or the spirit world? Keep your intention in mind as you stir the ingredients.

(1) Mix everything together in your cauldron.

(2) Place in a sealed glass jar and label it.

(3) Light a charcoal disc and wait until it turns grey around the edges – this should take about five minutes.

(4) Using tongs, drop the disc into an incense burner or any heatproof dish.

(5) Put a generous amount of your mixture onto the disc. It will release its spell-binding aroma at once.

MID-JANUARY TO MID-MARCH

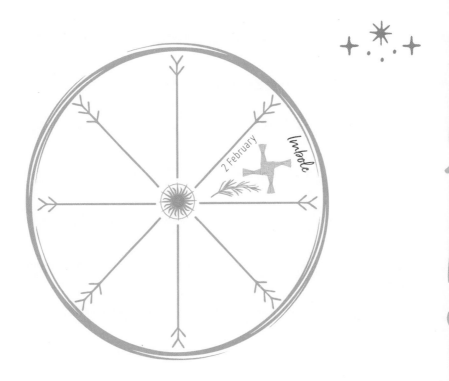

2 February

Imbolc

Sabbat of Imbolc:
2 February*

Imbolc: the darkest days are over; the earth is preparing to burst into life.

February can be a cold, bleak month, with rain dampening your spirits and cold winds whipping you quickly indoors. Embrace the moment and enjoy the chance to rest, pause and wonder. It is a good time to stay inside and bury yourself in weaving spells and making potions, but do not miss the first stirrings of life outdoors. Fresh shoots of nettle and wild garlic start to appear beneath your feet and remind you that this is the turning point of winter; the darkest days are over and spring is on its way.

The sabbat of Imbolc, held on 2 February*, is the half-way point between the winter solstice (the longest night of the year) and the spring equinox (21 March). It is a festival of fire, purification and new beginnings. *Imbolc* is a Celtic word that means 'in the belly' or 'in the womb'. This is a reference to the imminent birth of lambs, and more generally to seeds growing in Mother Earth, preparing for germination, waiting to burst into life.

The element of fire is the element of creation. The fire festival of Imbolc is a time to forge exciting projects in the furnace of winter. Bring fire and light into winter darkness by surrounding yourself with candles (the Christian festival at this time is called Candlemas), or light a bonfire and listen to it crackle and watch its flames. As it burns, let go of the past and think about how you would like to see your future. What changes will you make to refresh your life? You could start with spring cleaning and purifying your home. It is also the time to celebrate Brigid, the Irish Celtic goddess of fire, fertility, crops, poetry and the home.

* In the northern hemisphere, Imbolc falls on or around 2 February. If you are in the southern hemisphere, it will be on or around 1 August.

On your Imbolc altar

Be inspired by Brigid, who is often shown wearing a crown of flames, and add extra candles to your altar. As we are still in the middle of winter, place white candles (representing snow) in a circle, and in the centre put a Brigid Cross (see *Make a Brigid Cross* later in this chapter). Sprinkle pine needles around for grounding, and add herbs. Try bay leaves for wishes, thyme for healing and rosemary for remembrance. Add a crystal and a glass of milk for fertility and motherhood.

THE GODDESS

Worship of the Goddess has been practised for thousands of years in many different faiths. Some of the earliest sculpted human figures to be found are 'Venus figures': naked female forms with exaggerated sexual parts. She is still central to many indigenous people's beliefs, and continues to be at the heart of witchcraft. The Goddess takes on many guises but always represents limitless fertility, never-ending love and the source of magical power. Her male partner is the horned god, and together they generate all life. In covens they are represented by the high priest and high priestess.

Some goddesses, like Brigid (see *A Celtic Goddess*), are three-in-one: the virgin, the mother and the crone – the different aspects of femininity. During the course of the year, she takes on these different forms. At Imbolc, she is in her maiden form, barely stirring in sleep after giving birth to the sun at the winter solstice. By the time of the summer solstice and the harvest, she is in her mother form, and, as the year draws to a close at Samhain, she is the crone.

Celebrating the Goddess is an important part of modern witchcraft. It bolsters and liberates the power of women, nurtures our innermost selves and honours all our female ancestors.

Goddess guide

All of these goddesses embody feminine power and wisdom. Choose one that chimes with your wishes and aspirations, then channel her spirit and wisdom in rituals and spells by working with her symbols.

Aphrodite: beautiful Greek goddess of love, fertility and pleasure, who was brought to life borne on the waves of the ocean. Her Roman equivalent is Venus. *Symbols:* swans, roses, doves, sparrows.

Athena: the Greek goddess of war, wisdom and the home who sprung to life wearing armour. A fearless warrior. *Symbols:* owls, olive trees, snakes.

Bastet: Ancient Egyptian cat or lioness, goddess of pregnant women, childbirth and children. Also protects against disease and evil spirits. *Symbol:* the cat.

Cerridwen: the Celtic 'Great Mother Hen' of fertility, the moon, magic and astrology. *Symbols:* a stalk of wheat, a cauldron, an egg.

Demeter: Greek goddess of the harvest and agriculture. *Symbols:* wheat, bread, poppies.

Diana: fearless Greek goddess of the hunt and wild animals. *Symbols:* bow and arrow, the crescent moon, deer, dogs.

Freya: Nordic goddess of all things feminine: love, beauty, sex, fertility, divination and magic. *Symbols:* the triple spiral, a golden chariot pulled by cats, a hare.

Gaia: Greek goddess of the Earth. The personification of Mother Earth. *Symbols:* the earth, fruit, trees.

Hecate: the Greek goddess of witchcraft, the night, herbs and poisonous plants and the underworld. Often depicted as having three faces. *Symbols:* dogs, serpents, a dagger, garlic.

Inanna: Ancient Mesopotamian goddess of love, beauty, youth and spring. *Symbols:* the eight-pointed star, a lion, the rosette, a dove.

Isis: Egyptian goddess of magic and the moon. *Symbols:* the scorpion, birds, a cow, the tyet (a knot symbol with a loop at the top, similar to an ankh).

Lakshmi: Hindu goddess of purity and wealth. *Symbols:* rice, coins, a lotus flower, elephants, basil.

Pachamama: South American fertility goddess, who watches over the harvest and controls earthquakes. *Symbols:* the snake, wheat, fruit, butterflies, flowers.

Parvarti: Hindu goddess of love, femininity and devotion. *Symbols:* the lotus, elephants, red flowers.

Persephone: Greek goddess, queen of the underworld. *Symbols:* the pomegranate, lily of the valley, lavender, parrots and other talking birds.

Seshat: Ancient Egyptian librarian goddess of accountancy, architecture, astronomy, writing and maths. *Symbols:* leopard skin, stars, a pen, a notebook.

A Celtic goddess: Brigid

Fearless and powerful, Brigid is an Irish Celtic goddess who has been worshipped since Pre-Christian times, said to have been born at dawn's first light wearing a crown of fire. (The name Brigid means 'Fiery Arrow' or 'Bright One' in the ancient Celtic language.) Brigid is still with us today, becoming more and more visible as she is rediscovered by a new generation of neo-pagans and witches. She is the goddess of many things: fire and blacksmithing, springs, fertility, poetry, the home and hearth, childbirth and crops and livestock, among others.

When Christianity replaced pagan worship, Brigid was adopted by the church and became St. Bridgit, or Bride. Many sacred springs were reinvented as holy wells and dedicated to her, becoming places of healing and pilgrimage.

Offerings and rituals associated with Brigid are carried out on Imbolc, which is also Brigid's Day. As a goddess of fire, she is celebrated with a fire festival. Purification and cleansing rituals are especially effective now, drawing on her powers as goddess of the home as we prepare the house for spring.

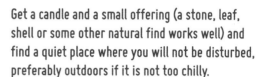

A SIMPLE GODDESS RITUAL

Get a candle and a small offering (a stone, leaf, shell or some other natural find works well) and find a quiet place where you will not be disturbed, preferably outdoors if it is not too chilly.

Light the candle and imagine Brigid, goddess of fire, dancing in its flames. Stand with your feet planted firmly on the ground, spaced slightly apart, and your arms stretched above your head, raised towards the sky.

Say aloud or in your head: "Brigid (or another goddess of your choosing), I am standing here before you, to honour your power and the power of all women. I come to thank you, and all the goddesses through all the centuries, for your wisdom and your guidance."

Place your offering on the ground in front of the candle, then say: "I give you this to show my gratitude and to celebrate your knowledge and creativity. Thank you for sharing it with all women."

Kneel in front of the candle, then blow it out, picturing your thanks dispersing into the sky towards the goddess.

IMBOLC PLANTS FOR REMEDIES AND SPELLS

Every plant that makes an appearance, pushing through the snow or battling against boggy conditions or nippy winds, is precious at this time of year. Alongside evergreen shrubs and herbs, the first signs of spring appear with the cheering arrival of snowdrops and hellebores. Although there are slim pickings for herbal remedies, any of these early sightings make joyful additions to your altar.

Snowdrop *(Galanthus):* One of the first wildflowers to appear at the edge of winter – even poking through snow – the snowdrop is a hopeful sign when everything else looks bleak. Seeing its spiky green leaves and nodding flowers reassures us that warmer days will return. Despite being a bringer of cheer, the snowdrop was traditionally regarded as an unlucky omen and considered to bring bad luck into the home. Some country people even thought it could turn milk watery and stop hens laying. This may be due to the fact that it is poisonous: do not include snowdrops in any remedies or potions, but do place a bunch on your Imbolc altar to represent the promise of spring.

Hellebore *(Helleborus):* Like snowdrops, hellebores flower when little else does. With beautiful, open flowers that dip their heads forwards as though they are looking at their shoes, they come in many colours, including yellow, white and pink. The most bewitching of all, however, is a deep maroon/black. Thriving in cold conditions, flowering in the shadows and with striking yellow stamens, these darker blooms have been prized by witches who, it is said, once dried the flowers and sprinkled the powder over themselves to become invisible. There are also tales of hellebore being used in flying ointments. Both of these uses must be avoided by the modern witch, however, as the plant is poisonous – even handling it can sting.

Dandelion root: Dandelion flowers, resembling yellow sunbursts, will not appear until May or June, when they shine out from hedgerows or pepper suburban lawns. Their roots, however, are at their sweetest now and can be dug up and added to soups or infused for teas. A dandelion-root infusion was once regarded as a powerful tonic and used to cure ailments such as jaundice and kidney complaints. It was also used as a cleansing drink and to generally aid digestion. The plant certainly has high levels of potassium and vitamins A, B, C and D. Its young, fresh leaves are also good in salads if a drink from the root does not appeal.

Rowan (*Sorbus):* One of the most magical of all trees, the Rowan is sacred to Brigid and associated with the maiden aspect of the Triple Goddess. This is because of its clusters of bright red berries that sing out at this time of year, and because the bottom of each berry has a tiny five-pointed star – a pentagram. Its twigs, with or without berries, can be brought indoors to protect the home. Some witches think that a rowan tree is a portal to the underworld. This is especially likely when they grow beside a stone circle, which they often do.

Witch ways: Try some of the following witchy ways to bring the power of Imbolc's plants into your home.

- Fasten a sprig of rowan or hang a bundle of rowan twigs near your front door to protect it. Even better, plant a tree in the garden outside, near the house.
- Float a single hellebore bloom face up in a bowl of water and place it on your altar to really enjoy its dark, gothic beauty.
- Pouring hot water over a bowlful of dandelion roots is said to help you reach the spirit world.
- Carry a bunch of snowdrops from room to room on Imbolc morning for a type of purification known as the White Cleansing.
- Place a bundle of dried rowan berries in a white cloth and tie with a purple ribbon. Hung in the kitchen, it is said to deter the flu.

ROWAN

CRYSTALS FOR IMBOLC

The first stirrings of nature are reflected in the crystals you choose during spring. Stones associated with beginnings, protection and dream work feel powerful now:

Turquoise: a heavenly talisman of azure-blue. The bewitching colour of this stone is a lot like that of the spring sky when the clouds part and the sun breaks through. Turquoise has been prized as a holy stone and a talisman through the centuries – the Aztecs, Persians, Ancient Egyptians and Native Americans all used it as adornment to bring power and luck, and for divination and prophesy. In modern witchcraft, it is valued for protection during vision quests or more mundane travel, and for providing comfort for those suffering from depression, or who are plagued by useless regrets. Allow it to soothe you and lift your spirits.

Amethyst: a healing stone of bewitching purple. Ranging in colour from pale lilac to an intense purple, this semi-precious stone is a type of quartz and is highly valued. The birthstone of February, it is associated with St. Valentine, who was thought to have worn an amethyst ring. The Ancient Greeks believed it helped to prevent drunkenness as its colour resembled wine. The modern witch uses it in healing rituals and to still the mind during meditation. It is also effective when used to create a magic circle. Placing it between the eyes is thought to stimulate the third eye chakra, which in turn strengthens imagination, intuition and personal power.

Black onyx: white fingernails in a jet-black crystal. This crystal has a seductively witchy vibe, especially when you realize that the white stripes that run through it resemble claws – 'onyx' is derived from the Greek *onuk*, which means fingernail. Dull when extracted, it polishes up beautifully, becoming glass-like: some witches use it for scrying. It is a powerful protection stone that can defend against negativity – put it in your pocket if you are heading towards a potentially combative situation. Use black onyx in rituals around Brigid, another protector, to keep super safe.

Moonstone: a glowing hot line to female energy. When polished, this opalescent, milky stone with its blue-white sheen has a lunar glow, which accounts for its name. It links powerfully to female energy and is associated with triple goddesses such as Brigid. A useful aid to clairvoyance, moonstone is most powerful when used in conjunction with the moon's waxing phases and will help tune your intuition and psychic centres. Hold it in both hands or keep near during meditation to ground and centre you. Moonstone is said to attract love: it is a traditional wedding gift in India.

CLEANSE AND CHARGE YOUR CRYSTALS

To keep your crystals active and alive, it is important to keep them free of dirt and dust.

To cleanse most crystals used for witchcraft, you can simply immerse them in warm, soapy water and brush away any dirt with a soft toothbrush. Rinse with clean water and dry with a soft cloth. Do this as a matter of course before using in a ritual or spell.

To charge a crystal to increase its potency, light a sage smudge stick (see *Beltane: Make a smudge stick*), then hold it in your non-dominant hand and grasp the stone in the other. Move the stone through the sage smoke for about 30 seconds, then extinguish the smudger.

Alternatively, sit the stone in the light of the moon – preferably placing it directly on the earth on the full moon – and leave for a night.

IMBOLC TRADITIONS AND CUSTOMS

Most of the traditions at Imbolc are to do with Brigid, particularly in her role as protector of the home. There are several more that are concerned with cleansing and purifying the home, and one or two others that combine all of these aspects.

Visiting a sacred spring, holy well or river

Traditionally this is the time of year to seek out a watery place for help and guidance and to wash away any darkness that lingers from the previous year. In Ireland, there is a tradition of visiting wells dedicated to St. Brigid, dipping a piece of cloth in its water and hanging it on a nearby tree or bush. Each of these 'clootie rags' is imbued with a prayer of hope or healing. A piece of silver, like a coin or a pin, is inserted into the wall of the well or thrown down into it as a gesture of thanks.

Witch way: if you do not have a well or spring nearby, head to a river or stream. If the water is clean, splash some on your hands and face, dab a little onto your third eye chakra in the middle of your forehead, and make an intention for the year ahead. Even better, take a dip and immerse yourself fully.

Welcoming Brigid into the home

In Ireland and the Scottish Highlands, Brigid was said to roam about on Imbolc, or St. Brigid's Eve, riding a sacred white cow and blessing farms and homes. Strips of cloth or ribbon were hung outside the door for her to bless. This piece of cloth was then used for healing throughout the year. In Scotland, as the cloth was hung, this invocation was spoken:

> *May Brigid give blessing to the house that is here*
>
> *Brigid, the fair and tender*
>
> *Her hue like the cotton-grass*
>
> *Rich-tressed maiden of ringlets of gold*

Witch way: before going to bed on Imbolc Eve, leave a small but special piece of clothing outside your house for Brigid to bless as she passes. If the mood takes you, chant the above invocation. In the morning, bring the item of clothing inside: it will be infused with powers of healing and protection.

Brigid dolls

In Ireland, it was traditional to make a cloth Brigid doll, usually dressed in white and green, carrying a white wand and accessorized with ribbons, lace and jewellery. On Imbolc Eve, children took the doll from door to door in exchange for milk, cheese and butter. The doll was also placed in a bed, and an offering of bread and milk was left out for Brigid. Once the doll was in place, the women went outside and said: "Brigit, Brigit, come in. Thy bed is ready." The following morning, the doll was taken from the bed and kept near the fire or hung near the door for protection and to aid childbirth. The next year it was burned in the fire and replaced with a new doll.

IMBOLC RITUALS AND SPELLS

This is a good time to clean your home and get rid of any clutter that has been bugging you. A cleaning ritual will help you banish stagnant energy, dispel anything heavy hanging around and get the house looking clean, uncluttered and ready to welcome the year ahead.

Simple solo sweeping ritual

It is easy to dismiss sweeping as yet another chore, but it is more than that. It has the power to shift negative energy and prepare the ground for better things. Many religious practices begin ceremonies by sweeping the holy space, and witches often sweep the floor before casting a magic circle.

For a special Imbolc sweep, take a broom and begin at the front porch. Either use your usual broom, keep one especially for spiritual sweeping and decorate it with symbols and ribbons, or make your own besom (see *Ostara: Make your own besom*). Rather than sweep the actual floor clear of dust, sweep the air above it. Treat this as a meditation and as you go, chant (either in your head or out loud): "I am sweeping away the bad so that the good will come in." This simple act symbolizes the importance of letting go of the past and making room for new, better things.

A simple snow spell

When it snows, do not just watch from inside — go outdoors before it disappears. Write wishes, hopes or symbols for the year ahead in the snow with a stick (a hazel stick would be good for this).

If it snows on St. Valentine's Day and you are looking for love, take this opportunity to cast a love spell in the snow. As the words melt, picture their energies drifting off into the universe as your desires begin to manifest.

An Imbolc Fire ritual with your witchy crew

Cast your magic circle (see *Summer Solstice: The Magic Circle*). Place a pile of wood that includes part, or all, of your old Christmas tree inside the circle. If you no longer have the tree, use any wood you can find. Gather your friends and each hold a candle. Preferably this takes place outdoors at night, but if that is impossible, cluster around your cauldron in place of the magic circle, and place twigs from the tree inside it.

You say: "At this time when the path ahead until Beltane is less dark, let us make a feast of torches to celebrate Brigid, the fire goddess, keeper of the sacred flame and guardian of home and hearth."

You light the wood or branches and say: "Light now your flames from the sacred fire."

Going around the circle, each person approaches the fire and lights their candle from it.

They hold their candles up high in their left hand and say: "We honour Brigid, sun-dazzling goddess, splendid and fearless."

You say: "As the old wood burns, our worries vanish into the air, to be replaced with Brigid's strength. We celebrate the courage of Brigid and thank her for her protection on our journey in the forthcoming year."

Everyone says: "We honour Brigid, sun-dazzling, splendid and fearless."

You say: "So mote it be."

Everyone says: "So mote it be."

The candles are placed around the fire and left to burn out. Remember to keep an eye on them and make sure they are extinguished. The circle is unwound. Everyone celebrates with feasting and music.

WITCHY CRAFT

MAKE A BRIGID CROSS

In Ireland, this ancient Celtic symbol was traditionally made on Imbolc and left outside the house for Brigid to bless. It would protect the house all year, and was then burned or tucked up in the rafters of the house to be replaced with a new one.

There are many different forms of a Brigid Cross (or *cros Bride* as it is known in Gaelic). The one described here is the simplest and most common. Other forms include a lozenge-shape, a three-legged cross and a U-shape. In the past, the cross was made from either wheat straw or rushes. The rushes were pulled from the ground (not cut) during the day on 31 January, then brought into the house with great ceremony. These days, crosses are made from many different sorts of material and their design can be complicated and highly decorative. This simple cross not only represents Brigid but it is symbolic of the turning of the wheel of the year, and each leg represents a different quarter, i.e. north, south, east and west.

If you want to stick with tradition, finding and collecting rushes can be incorporated into a mindful walk or meditation. If that is out of the question, though, you could use paper straws and tie the ends with rubber bands. When finished, the cross should look like a central woven square with four protruding arms tied at their ends. Hang it over a door or a window to protect your home and its occupants.

WHAT YOU NEED

• about 15 rushes approximately 10–12cm long; alternatively, use paper drinking straws

• string or rubber bands to tie the ends

Making your Brigid cross

Follow these simple steps.

1 Hold one rush/straw in the centre and pinch it.

2 Fold it around another rush/straw to form a T shape.

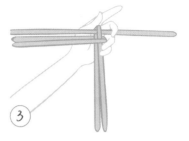

3 Pinch another rush/straw in the centre. Place it beneath the first and fold as shown. Hold both rushes in one hand.

4 Rotate one quarter.

5 Pinch another rush/straw in the centre. Place to form the fourth arm of the cross.

6 Hold on to it, rotate back again and add another pinched rush/straw.

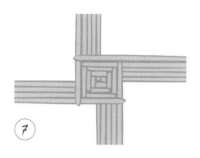

7 Repeat until you have a reasonably sized square shape at the centre.

8 Tie each arm with string or rubber bands to hold everything in place.

9 Trim the straws at each end to keep the arms tidy.

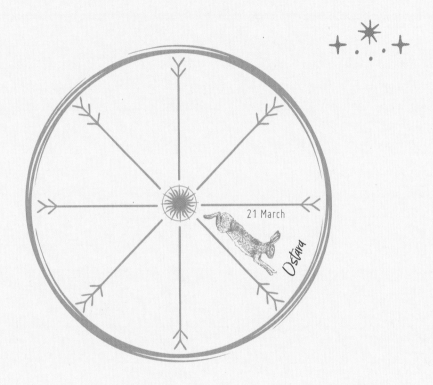

21 March

Ostara

Sabbat of Ostara, the Spring Equinox: 21 March*

The Spring Equinox: the first day of Spring. Germination begins. A time of powerful energetic release.

There is much magic in the air and in the earth at this time of year. Nature stirs all around as new growth, buried until now, reveals itself. Fresh lime-green leaves unfurl from trees; seeds push their shoots up through the ground; and wild animals prepare their nests for the arrival of their young. On farms, livestock grow plump as they get ready to give birth. The world is coming alive, emerging from the grip of winter. Spring is finally here.

The spring (vernal) equinox, falling around 21 March* and also known as Ostara, enjoys days and night of equal length. This is when the sun passes over the equator on its journey from south to north. The light is returning as the wheel of the year revolves; it is a time of new beginnings. The word 'Ostara' is German, but originates from the name of an Anglo-Saxon goddess called Esotre, who was celebrated with a festival that lasted several days. This festival was adopted by Christians as Easter (which falls on the full moon following the spring equinox). In Druid traditions, it is known as *Alban Ellir* – light of the earth.

The modern witch embraces the potential everywhere. It is a time to plant seeds and prepare for growth. This could be the simple act of planting herbs in a pot on a windowsill. It could be the development of your inner witch by creating spells, potions and rituals. Or it could be making plans to change direction in your career or personal life. There is expansive and exuberant energy all around now. It would be a shame to waste it.

* In the Northern Hemisphere, the spring equinox falls on or around 21 March. If you are in the Southern Hemisphere, it will be on or around 21 September.

On your spring equinox altar:

Your altar should brim with the fresh loveliness of spring. See if you can find some twigs with unfurling leaves or blossom and put them in a vase. Surround this with other flowers or a pot full of bulbs, bursting into life. Create a little 'nest' in a bowl with straw or twigs, and fill with decorated eggs. Add an ornamental hare (buy, draw or make one) and crystals that have meaning to you at this time. And do not forget a few candles or tea lights. Yellow, purple and green candles – the colours of new growth in nature – are good now.

MAGICAL CREATURES

The bond between witches and animals is strong. Many witches keep animals, and they are an important part of their lives. Some also have 'animal spirit guides' with whom they communicate, and who offer spiritual guidance. From the Native American tradition, spirit animals are seen as teachers or messengers who offer help and support. Witches choose an animal that has particular meaning to them. In Medieval times, many witches were said to have 'familiars': animal assistants who helped them carry out sorcery and malevolent practices (see below and overleaf).

Spring, when many creatures give birth, is a good time to think about animals, their presence in our lives and their magical qualities. While all animals are valued as part of the natural world, and as our companions who share the planet with us, there are some that have particular power and magic.

Hare

Seeing one of these elusive creatures can be tricky – modern farming practices have led to a decline in numbers. But get up an hour after dawn and head to a wheat field, and you may see one bounding gracefully before you, powered by its mighty hind legs, its ears tipped with black, its eyes flashing. Mostly nocturnal and silent, it is a creature of the shadows, but 'boxing hares' (a female rebuffing an amorous male) can be seen in March if you are lucky. Many magical associations surround the hare: in England, witches were thought to disguise themselves as hares. Stories exist of a hare turning into a crone when the hunters turned the hounds on it. The Chinese found the hare so otherworldly that they imagined it had descended from the moon. It is still a lunar symbol and, as it can conceive while pregnant, is symbolic of fertility and abundance.

Toad

Do not be fooled by the warty appearance of the toad, or by the glands on its skin that secrete poison when it is provoked. Under this unattractive exterior is a benign and lovable creature who should be treated with respect. Remember the fairy tale of the ugly toad who turned into a handsome prince when kissed. In Medieval times, however, the toad was regarded as a creature of the Devil, and witches were thought to include it in potions: toad's spittle was combined with thistle sap to conjure invisibility. Toads were also said to be kept as familiars, sent out to cause mischief, mishaps and mayhem, and hopped on witches' broomsticks as they rode to sabbats. Modern witches think of toads in a more kindly light: some keep them as pets, noting that they are intelligent and easy to tame and care for. A toad is also a symbol of fortune, fertility and abundance.

Cat

Witchy women and their feline companions have a particular bond. The sleek and stealthy cat can be incredibly friendly and companionable some of the time, but can then be distant and unknowable at other times. These characteristics, combined with its natural elegance and grace, have meant the cat has been linked with the supernatural since ancient times. During the Middle Ages, cats were thought to embody the Devil and were consequently hunted and burned as witches' familiars, often appearing in witch trials with names like Sathan and Pyewackett. There are countless superstitions surrounding black cats: it is considered good luck to own one, but if one crosses your path, then that means bad luck. A broth made from a black cat was an unlikely cure for consumption, and sometimes charms made from a cat's whiskers were even crafted - these were thought to bring misfortune to a victim.

Owl

With its flat face, revolving head and chilling cry, the owl flies low across the land, mysterious, spooky and magical. As it flies, it silently surveys the ground for prey before dropping from the air, its talons outstretched in readiness for the kill. Perhaps its predilection for nightly hunting earned the owl its reputation as a bird associated with death, sorcery and darkness. To the Ancient Egyptians it represented night, death and cold. The Romans saw it as a bad omen, and its screeching was a sign that death was imminent. Ancient Greeks, however, viewed it as a symbol of wisdom – an owl is the constant companion of the Goddess Athena. In the UK, barn owls were once known as the Bird of Doom, and if you saw one during the day, it meant you would receive bad news. These days, it is always a good thing to see an owl in the wild: this charismatic, ghostly creature never fails to enchant.

Fox

Usually out at night, dashing out of sight behind a tree or around a corner as we approach, the fox is known for its cleverness and wits. A trickster that transforms to suit its surroundings, whether that is the town or the country, it evades our efforts to domesticate it. In many European fairy and folk tales, the fox outsmarts humans and other animals. During the Middle Ages, its cunning and nocturnal activities linked it with the Devil in superstitious minds, whereas the Celtic people (and some Native Americans) believed it to be a guide or a wise messenger. Best to see it as a teacher to guide you through the darkness, and to help sharpen your own wit and adaptability.

Familiars

The history of witches' familiars is a dark one. During the Middle Ages, animals including cats, toads, owls, mice and even flies, were said to be shapeshifters that transformed into demons, used by witches to assist with spells and bewitchments. During the English witchcraft trials in the 16th century, animals were used as evidence to condemn women as witches — a pet cat was proof that its owner was skilled in the practice of magic. Witchfinders, who tried, tortured and executed women for witchcraft, thought that familiars assisted witches in all manner of devilish activities. These days, we see animals as companions, spirit guides and, possibly, possessing psychic powers.
None are believed to be inhabited by the Devil.

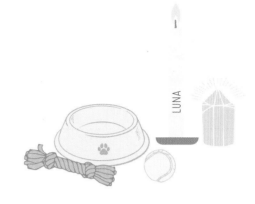

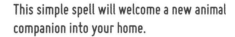

A WELCOME SPELL

This simple spell will welcome a new animal companion into your home.

Witch way: Before your new pet arrives, place a piece of rose quartz next to an item you bought for them such as a collar, food bowl or toy – anything they will be closely associated with. Find a long white candle and carve your new pet's name into it with a knitting needle or small penknife. Include any other words or symbols you like.

Place the candle in a holder by the pet's item and the rose quartz. Light the candle, and as it burns, imagine a beam of love pouring out from your heart into the crystal, then into the object. When you have filled them with love, blow the candle out. If there's any candle left, keep it to top up the love at a later date.

SPRING PLANTS FOR REMEDIES AND SPELLS

The first blooms of spring are mostly modest and unassuming. They appear sprinkled across the woodland floor, puncturing the shadows with pretty clusters of flowers. Despite their demure appearance, these plants have plenty to offer the witch, from refreshing teas to scented pillows and ingredients for foraged meals.

Daffodil *(Narcissus):* The bright yellow flowers of daffodils are one of the first to bloom in spring and sing out from road verges and gardens with a cheery hello. A bunch is a welcome addition to a spring altar. It is a flower associated with romance and fertility: a single daffodil worn close to your heart is thought to attract love; traditionally, a vase of daffs was placed beside a bed to encourage pregnancy. Daffodils are also thought to improve your luck. Spot the first one to bloom in your garden and good fortune will follow.

Borage *(Borago officinalis):* Easy to grow and loved by bees, this tall, sturdy plant with bright-blue flowers is a fine addition to any witch's kitchen garden. At this time of year, star-shaped flowers appear on its hairy, tubular stems, attracting masses of flying insects busy collecting its pollen. Gather its leaves now when the plant is in flower by stripping them off the stem one by one. A tea made from dried leaves has a slight cucumber flavour and is said to boost psychic powers. Add the flowers to a jug filled with water, lemon and sugar for a pretty, cooling drink.

Bluebell *(Hyacinthoides):* The drifts of bluebells that appear in woodland from mid-April have a magic all of their own. The bell-shaped flowers with their rolled-back tips hang on drooping stems, resembling fairies' bonnets, and there are many legends linking them with fairy folk. The stories go that at dawn, for example, fairies were summoned back to safety from where they had been sleeping in the woods by the bells of the flower ringing. If a human heard the bells, on the other hand, they would be visited by a bad fairy and die. A swathe of English bluebells (which are scented and smaller than the invasive Spanish bluebell) is also an indicator of ancient woodland.

> **A word of warning:** Daffodils are highly toxic, and they should never be used medicinally or ingested in any way.

Wild garlic *(Allium ursinum):* Another inhabitant of the wood – where all magical things are found – wild garlic starts to appear in early March. Do not mistake its broad, spear-shaped leaves for the narrower ones of Lily of the Valley or Lords and Ladies: both of these are poisonous. Crush a leaf in your hand, and if it smells garlicky, you will know what's what. A couple of weeks after the leaves show, white star-shaped flowers appear in clusters, peppering the woodland floor. All parts of the plant, including its bulb, can be eaten (although you should not dig it up; just take the leaves) and are good in a pesto, with pasta or added to soup. Your immune system and intestines will thank you for it. Its reputation as a cure-all, and its power to help skin conditions, has earned it the name The Fountain of Youth by the Romany people.

Witch ways: Here are some ways to make the most of this season's plants. See *A Witch's Herbal* for directions on drying herbs and making infusions.

- Scattering a few daffodils into your bath is said to bring you greater amounts of luck and attract new people into your life.

- Pin a sprig of borage to your coat if you are heading outdoors. It is said to give you courage and protection when walking.

- To bring good fortune, put a bluebell in your shoe while saying: "Bluebell, bluebell, bring me some luck before tomorrow night."

- An old Irish tradition involved planting wild garlic in the thatched roofs of cottages to ward off fairies and bring good luck.

WILD GARLIC

CRYSTALS FOR OSTARA

As Ostara is about all things fresh and new, pick crystals that will help develop your creativity, aid cleansing or purification rituals or encourage new ways of looking and behaving. Here are some suggestions, but if they do not work for you, it does not matter; choose ones that you feel a connection with.

Jasper: sacred, powerful stone of Isis.
This elemental Earth stone was revered by the Ancient Egyptians, who associated it with the blood of Isis, carved amulets from it and buried it to accompany their dead to the afterlife. The indigenous people of America valued it as a tool to bring rain and to dowse for water. Although most commonly red, jasper comes in a variety of colours, including black, blue, brown and even striped. The rarest form is ocean jasper, found in Madagascar. Jasper is powerful now, when the Goddess awakens. It prompts creativity and can help you develop new projects. It is said that holding and rubbing jasper can soothe nerves and banish nightmares.

Serpentine: the coiled potential of a snake.
This speckled green stone is associated with the snake (its name is from the Latin *serpentinus*, which means 'resembling a serpent'). In yogic traditions, the coiled snake is a form of divine feminine energy, called *kundalini* in Sanskrit and located at the base of the spine, which can be released through spiritual practices. It helps you to access your deeper consciousness and is good for clearing psychic energy blockages and to keep beside you during meditation.

Citrine: a sunbeam in solid form.
This lovely clear quartz ranges from a pale lemon colour, through golden honey to brown. It radiates positive energy and joyfulness and is as warm and comforting as a sunbeam. Some call it the 'stone of the mind' and recommend placing it on the third eye chakra at your brow to increase psychic powers. Also known as 'the merchant's stone', it is said to attract money. Keep a piece in your purse to help manifest wealth, or place it on your grid (see *Crystals for Samhain: Design a crystal grid*) to clear the mind and awaken your imagination.

Lapis lazuli: the starry sky in your hand.
This celestial-blue stone is shot through with flecks of gold and violet. Its intense colour and rarity have been valued since ancient times. It was worn as jewellery by Ancient Egyptians pharaohs and queens, who saw it as a symbol of gods, royalty and power. More recently, it has been used to decorate important places: Catherine the Great's palace in St. Petersburg, the Taj Mahal in India and the ceiling of the Sistine Chapel in Vatican City, among others. It is also a powerful spiritual stone, used in dream and vision work and to contact spirit guides. Place it close to your bed or under a pillow as you sleep, and see what happens.

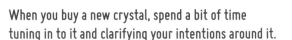

CONSECRATING NEW CRYSTALS

When you buy a new crystal, spend a bit of time tuning in to it and clarifying your intentions around it.

First, cleanse the crystal's energy using a smudge stick (see *Beltane: Make a smudge stick*): light the bundle of sage, then pass the crystal through its smoke. Hold the crystal in both hands held out in front of you and speak to it. Tell it why you have chosen it, what you hope it will bring and how you intend to use it. Thank it for coming into your life. Your crystal is then ready to use in whichever way you choose.

OSTARA TRADITIONS AND CUSTOMS

Many of the ways the Christian festival of Easter is celebrated have their origins in pagan or Druidic customs. As a modern witch, you can work with this blending of beliefs, customizing traditions and rituals to suit your own practice.

The Easter Bunny

At this time of year, you cannot avoid rabbits in the shops. There are chocolate ones, fluffy soft toy ones, ceramic ones shaped like egg cups and anything else you can think of! The cheeky Easter Bunny has become knitted into the fabric of Easter celebrations. Where this originated is uncertain, but it may have come from ancient reverence for the hare. To birth its young, known as leverets, this lunar animal (see *Magical Creatures*) creates a shelter, called a form, in a depression in the soil. The form is often lined with fur, which the mother plucks from her own coat. Once the leverets leave their birthplace, partridges and pheasants sometimes lay their eggs in the empty form. This may account for the association of hares/rabbits and eggs at springtime. The hare is nocturnal, with a gestation period of 28 days (the length of a lunar cycle) and a symbol of the moon.

Easter eggs

The egg is where life begins and as such has always been a powerful magical symbol. It symbolizes potential, promise, fertility and things yet to come: the perfect emblem for spring. In Christianity, the egg, with its hard exterior protecting embryonic life within, is associated with the resurrection of Jesus and his emergence from the tomb. Giving eggs at Easter goes further back than the advent of Christianity, however. The Chinese gave painted eggs as gifts at the beginning of spring around 5,000 years ago, and in Ancient Greece and Rome it was customary to hang decorated eggs to celebrate the March equinox. Placing a chocolate or decorated egg on your altar is a reminder of the potency and potential of this time of year.

Witch way: decorate some eggs to put on your altar. Empty the contents by making holes in either end – one larger than the other – and blowing through the small hole until everything comes out. Then either colour the eggs with a natural dye, or paint and decorate them with symbols and patterns that resonate with you.

Hot cross buns

Baking a spicy bun marked with a pastry cross is a Christian custom that marks the end of Lent. A 14th century monk from St. Albans is said to have started the tradition by baking buns to distribute to the poor on Good Friday, although they were not widely produced until the 17th century. The cross represents the crucifixion of Jesus, and the spices are said to signify those used to embalm him at his burial. Tucking into a freshly-baked bun was a welcome treat after days of fasting. Modern witches, who also like a warm pastry, could see the bun as a Celtic cross with four equal arms. Four is a potent number: it symbolizes the four sacred directions – north, east, south and west – that are acknowledged at the start of rituals. It is also the number of quarters of the moon and of the elements. The round circumference of the bun symbolizes the circle of life or the wheel of the year, with a still point at its centre.

Witch way: if making your own hot cross buns is too troublesome, buy some good-quality ones and warm them up. Eat, buttered preferably, as part of a ritual and reflect on what they symbolize.

OSTARA RITUALS AND SPELLS

Now is the time to celebrate fresh beginnings. Focus on the egg as a symbol of new life and organize egg hunts, or decorate a few and put them in a bowl. Sow herb seeds now to use the plants later in spells and remedies. Anticipate future growth, but do not forget to relish the new life all around you.

Simple solo spring ritual

Wake up early and go outside to greet the dawn. It may feel like a wrench to get out of bed, but it will be worth it! As the sun rises, feel its warmth on your face and watch its light change the colour of the sky and everything around you. Look for signs of spring: new shoots of bulbs, buds on trees, leaves unfurling. Listen for birdsong. Make an offering to the Goddess of Spring. This could be a cup of water or bowl of milk poured onto the earth. As you pour, think about what you want to grow this year – not just plants, but seeds that will improve your career, relationships or self-worth. Thank the Goddess for the gift of spring.

One easy thing: cook up a spring feast

After a ritual is over, continue the celebrations with a meal using fresh spring ingredients. A wild garlic omelette is a perfect, easy meal. Put a knob of butter into a frying pan and toss in a handful of wild garlic leaves (wash and chop them first). As they wilt, season with salt and pepper. Transfer to a plate. Add a splash of olive oil to the pan, and as it warms up, beat a couple of eggs in a bowl and season. Pour the eggs into the frying pan, tipping it to spread them evenly. When it looks as though the egg is setting, add the wild garlic — you could also add grated cheese for extra oomph. Fold in half and serve at once.

A simple spring equinox fertility ritual with your witchy crew

Cast your circle (see *Summer Solstice: The Magic Circle*). Gather your friends to stand around your altar, which should be freshly decorated with spring flowers, a small bowl filled with fresh soil and a large seed of some sort (a broad bean is good).

You (or another nominated person) say: "Welcome everyone. It is time to greet the spring. Light and dark are equal, and the earth begins to wake up from its slumber. We are here to celebrate Ostara, the spring equinox, and the growing light and the awakening life that is all around us."

Everyone says: "Welcome, welcome, beautiful spring!"

You say: "The sky fills with light; the sun warms the earth. Let us cast behind us the darkness of winter and look forward to what lies ahead. Now is the time for birth; now is the time for planting seeds."

You pick up the bowl of earth and say: "This is a joyful time for growth, when the world bursts into life around us. We celebrate this energy today by planting this seed."

Another person picks up the seed, puts it into the bowl, then covers it with soil. That person says: "I place this seed in the womb of the earth so that it will become a part of the earth, a part of life and a part of us."

You say: "Let love grow and flourish as the seed grows and flourishes. We are thankful that spring has come. We are blessed to be alive this day. Welcome, life! Welcome, light! Welcome spring!"

Everyone says: "Welcome, life! Welcome, light! Welcome spring!"

You say: "So mote it be."

Everyone says: "So mote it be."

You say: "This celebration of Ostara, the spring equinox, is complete. Hail and farewell."

The dish is placed on the altar. The circle is unwound Everyone celebrates with music, dancing and feasting.

WITCHY CRAFT

MAKE YOUR OWN BESOM (BROOMSTICK)

Nothing says 'witchiness' quite like a broomstick. Images of witches flying about on their broomsticks (or 'besoms'*) at full moon have become part of spooky folklore. The origins for the pairing of witches and their brooms are said to lie in a misguided Medieval preconception. It was thought that witches coated themselves with a hallucinatory ointment extracted from plants like mandrake or deadly nightshade (very poisonous: do not even think about it!), which prompted them to mount their broomsticks and leap or 'fly' around the countryside.

With a nod to her forebears, the modern witch uses her besom as part of a cleansing ritual before casting a circle. Held above the ground, it sweeps away negative energy and prepares the space for magic (see *Ostara: Simple solo sweeping ritual*).

*from the Old English, 'besma' meaning 'bundle of twigs'.

WHAT YOU NEED:

• a bundle of twigs

• strong twine and/or thin wire

• a sharp knife, scissors or secateurs

Making your besom

What you need to do:

(1)

Head off into the woods or local park and collect some twigs. Look for some about 2.5m long and as straight as possible. Twigs that fall from silver birch are good, but any of the right length will work.

(2)

Tie a length of good strong twine to a broom handle or a sturdy, straight branch of a similar length, about 10cm from the end.

(3)

Place a circle of twigs around the end of the broom handle and bind into place with the string, allowing about 10cm of the twigs to lie along the broom handle. Thin wire can also be used, but bind twine over it to finish it neatly.

(4)

Add another layer of twigs on top and bind them, too. Continue building the layers up until the broom is a good size, binding tightly as you go. You might like to add a final layer of twine at the end to make it look tidier and more finished.

(5)

Trim any unruly twigs, and you're ready to fly – metaphorically!

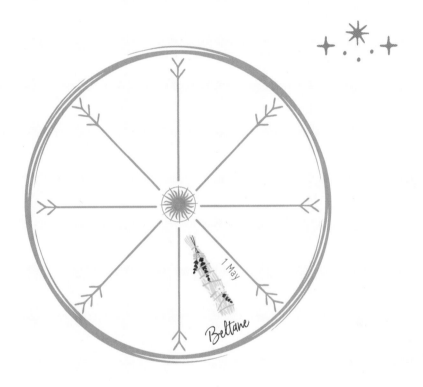

Sabbat of
Beltane: 1 May*

Beltane: a festival of fertility. Plants sprout rapid external growth. A time of development and learning.

This is the greenest time of year, when plants are at their best, and the world sparkles with life and promise. The sabbat of Beltane, which begins at moonrise on the eve of 1 May*, welcomes the summer and anticipates the abundance ahead. In earlier times, it was widely celebrated with fire: the word 'Beltane' means 'bright fire'. Bonfires were lit as they were believed to bring fertility to crops, homes and livestock. People danced *deosil* (clockwise) around the flames for good luck and protection against illness, and cattle were driven between fires or made to leap over the embers to protect them and keep them in good health.

Fairy spirits were thought to be particularly active at Beltane and roamed the country in great numbers. Many of these sprites were thought to be agents of misfortune, and it was unlucky to be out late at night on Beltane Eve in case you met one. Other, more kindly spirits were thought to live in trees that are in flower at this time of year, such as hawthorn (see *Beltane Plants for Remedies and Spells*). These trees were decorated with flowers and ribbons, and food was left out to appease the spirits, a tradition that continues today in parts of Ireland.

Beltane remains one of the most important sabbats for the modern witch, with rituals celebrating birth, fertility and the blossoming of all life taking place. Some witches honour the union of the Sun God and Goddess at this time. Others jump over broomsticks and dance around maypoles – both symbols of fertility. And some simply bring a bough of blossom into the home and revel in the beauty that this season brings.

* In the Northern Hemisphere, Beltane falls on or around 31 April. If you are in the Southern Hemisphere, it will be on or around 1 November.

On your Beltane altar

This is a joyful time of year, so decorate your altar with things that make you happy. Some blossom from a may tree (hawthorn) would be perfect, as would a few sunny dandelions in a jar filled with rainwater. Make a mini maypole from a stick and some coloured ribbons, and add a couple of matching candles. If you have a set of runes or a Tarot pack, choose a stone or card to include on your altar. And if you have made a smudge stick (see later in this chapter), add that as a blessing.

> **Word of warning:** make sure you keep candles well out of reach of any fluttering ribbons in case of fire.

RUNES AND THE TAROT

Runes

The origins of runes – cryptic symbols used for divination and healing – are mysterious and their purpose enigmatic. According to myth, they were created by Odin: the one-eyed god of wisdom and war hanged himself from the Tree of Life (Yggdrasil) for nine days and nights to receive their forbidden, mystical knowledge. Symbols appeared at the base of the tree, carved on pieces of wood.

It's more likely – though less appealing – that they originated in Scandinavia in the 2nd century AD and were characters used in an alphabet until the early 16th century. Nevertheless, they have long been held to possess magical qualities. (The common Germanic root of the word 'rune' is 'run', which meant 'mystery' or 'whisper' in Old Norse.)

During the Dark Ages in Western Europe, runes accrued magical power, and runic symbols were carved on to magicians' wooden wands or stone tablets. Since then, runic signs have been used for divination similar to the Tarot.

Each rune has a name, which may vary according to the translation used. In the above illustration from left to right, they are: feoh, ur, thorn, os, rad, cen, gifu, wyn, hegel, nead, is, gear, eoh, peorth, eolhx, sigel, tir, berc, eh, man, lagu, ing, daeg and epel.

MAKE YOUR OWN RUNES SET

By creating your own runes, you fill them with your energetic vibrations and get more accurate readings. There are several ways to do this:

- Collect stones or pebbles of a similar size. Paint a symbol on each, then seal with a matt varnish to prevent it from chipping off.

- Find a long straight branch. Strip off the bark, then saw widthways into discs. Mark the runes with paint or ink, or carve or burn the design into the wood.

- Make clay tablets of equal size. Decorate with the symbols, then fire in a kiln.

- If you are really dedicated, get hold of a piece of bone – part of an antler would do it. Saw into discs, carve the symbols into the bone, then fill in with ink.

Witch way: Once you have made your set, consecrate it with a small dedication – gather a small bowl of water, a candle and your runes. Light the candle, pick up a rune, dab a little water onto it with your finger and say its name. Pass the rune over the candle and say its name again. Repeat with the other tablets.

The Tarot

The 78 illustrated cards of the Tarot are one of the most valued and used divinatory tools of the modern witch. Some people are afraid of them because they have been associated with black magic, but, used properly and with respect, they can provide important insights. See the cards as an aid to self-empowerment, and they will lead you to discover the riches of trusting your intuition.

Like the runes, the origins and purpose of the Tarot are mysterious. The word 'tarot' is French, and the earliest record of the cards is around 1392 at the court of King Charles VI of France. Chances are, though, that they date much further back than that: they have been linked to the mystical teachings of Thoth, the Egyptian god of magic and healing. In the 18th century, they were championed by a French archaeologist who believed they were fragments from an ancient Egyptian book.

During the 15th century, the Roma people roamed Europe and claimed they inherited the cards from ancestors who found them in Egypt or Iraq.

The Tarot comprises two decks in one: the Major Arcana (see below) and the Minor Arcana (*arcana* is Latin for 'secrets'). The Major Arcana has 22 cards and reflects the important events in a person's life. Each card depicts a scene featuring a person or several people and has its own symbolic meaning. The story of the Tarot represents a journey, with The Fool representing the self and the other cards characters he meets along the way. The Minor Arcana, which has 56 cards, adds and expands details of the Major Arcana. It has four suits – Cups, Pentacles, Swords and Wands – which are the precursor of today's playing cards. Over time, they became the suits, hearts, spades, clubs and diamonds.

THE MAJOR ARCANA

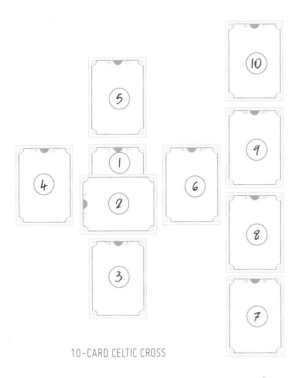

10-CARD CELTIC CROSS

KEY

card 1 – where you are right now

card 2 – potential challenges

card 3 – what to focus on

card 4 – your past

card 5 – your strengths

card 6 – near future

card 7 – suggested approach

card 8 – what you need to know

card 9 – hopes and fears

card 10 – your potential future

HOW TO READ THE TAROT

There are dozens of Tarot card packs to choose from, most of which are based on the Rider–Waite pack, created in 1910. Find one that speaks to you.

Witch way: To read the cards, you must first ask them a question. Think carefully about the words you use. Many witches use only the Major Arcana cards for simplicity. Lay the cards out in front of you. There are various patterns to choose from, from the very simple, such as a few cards in a line, to more complex arrangements. Pay attention to how the cards fall: whether they land right side up or 'reversed' (with the picture upside down); this will affect their meaning. Also notice how they relate to other cards in the spread. Let your intuition lead you and be open to what you find. The cards will answer your question and guide you.

Wrap your cards in a soft material like velvet or satin, and store them in a box. Always treat them with care.

BELTANE PLANTS FOR REMEDIES AND SPELLS

The earth is bursting with fertility now. Vivid green leaves curl from branches and flowering plants reach upwards and burst into bloom. This is the greenest and freshest time of year, when blossom froths and plants look their bewitching best.

Hawthorn *(Crataegus monognya):* This magical tree is covered with white blossom now, hence its alternative name, the may tree. A sign that spring is giving way to summer, it is a symbol of fertility and is used to decorate the maypole. Traditionally, May was the month of courtship and love. Young women rose at dawn to bathe in the dew found on hawthorn flowers to ensure their beauty in the coming year. In Ireland, the hawthorn is a fairy tree, a portal to the otherworld, especially when it grows beside a holy well or near a stone circle. Not everyone sees hawthorn in a good light, however: its sharp thorns and dense, twisted shape led some to believe that hawthorns were witches in tree form. Many people still will not bring it into the house, thinking that bad luck will follow.

Hyssop *(Hyssopus officinalis):* The leaves of this aromatic plant appear now (its spikes of blue flowers appear in summer and early autumn) and have been long valued for their culinary and medicinal use. Hyssop was especially popular in Tudor times, when it was used as a hedging plant (like we use box today) and in cooking, especially to flavour stews. Mentioned in the Bible for its purifying qualities, it is also used by the modern witch to purify a space before a ritual. The leaves can be used fresh as an infusion, or dried and burned, either in a smudge stick or simply on a ceramic dish.

Sage *(Salvia officinalis):* An old rhyme states that 'He that would live for aye, Must eat sage in May.' It is unlikely that a daily diet of sage will guarantee longevity, but it does have many other uses, both culinary and in magic. It is an essential ingredient for the modern witch, principally used in a smudge stick (see *Make a smudge stick* later in this chapter) to purify a space in preparation for magic work, but also as an infusion to ease digestion and calm the nerves. It is an easy herb to grow, so long as you plant it in a sunny, sheltered spot. It is evergreen, so you can pick its strongly scented leaves all year round. In the summer, sage is awash with purple-blue flowers, which look striking against its grey-green foliage.

Sweet Woodruff (*Gallium odoratum*): One of the traditional Beltane herbs, this pretty plant appears in May and sprinkles the forest floor with its star-shaped flowers. It can be tricky to find, so growing your own is the best way to ensure a supply. It will grow fast and abundantly once it gets going. In Medieval times, its sweet scent led to it being one of several plants used to stuff mattresses. Its alleged aphrodisiac properties mean that it is often used in handfasting ceremonies (see *Lughnasadh Traditions and Customs*). It can be drunk as an infusion or as a May Bowl (see *Witch ways*, opposite), but use in moderation: too much can cause dizziness and nausea.

Witch ways: Here are some ways you can reap the benefits of these seasonal plants. See *A Witch's Herbal* for directions on drying herbs.

- Hawthorn: carry a sachet of hawthorn blossom if you are feeling sad or depressed. It is said to perk up the troubled mind.

- Hyssop: tie a few sprigs of Hyssop to your besom (see *Ostara: Make your own besom*) and sweep away negative energy.

- Sage: fill a sleep sachet with dried leaves and place under your pillow. It will protect you from nightmares.

- Sweet Woodruff: make a celebratory May Bowl punch to serve at your Beltane gathering. Add two cups of washed flowers to eight cups of white wine. Pour into a sealed container and store in the fridge overnight. Next day, add a tablespoon of orange zest and sugar to taste. Strain and serve.

SWEET WOODRUFF

CRYSTALS FOR BELTANE

Gorgeous green feels right for this time of year but, as ever, when choosing crystals for your spells or to place on your Beltane altar, be led by your intuition. If you are working with more than one crystal, be aware of how they respond to each other as some are more comfortable in a pair than others. These feel powerful now:

Rose quartz: feminine energy beaming love.
This pale pink stone is all about love, reflecting the fertility and sexuality that abounds at this time of year. Called the Heart Stone, it is the one to choose if you want to attract new love, deepen an existing relationship or give yourself a little self love. Its soft, feminine energy was valued by the Ancient Egyptians (it has been found in many tombs), as well as by Tibetan and Oriental cultures. This compassionate and generous stone abounds, so is easy to find. You may be drawn to its rough, natural state, or prefer a polished or shaped crystal. Wear rose quartz in a pendant close to your heart to remind yourself of the power of love, and imagine it beaming from your heart centre to others.

Aventurine: glistening green fairy treasure.
Although it comes in various colours, it is the glistening green version of this stone that matches the leafy spirit of Beltane. Aventurine was sacred to the Ancient Tibetans, who used it for the eyes in their statues to symbolize visionary power. Known as 'fairy treasure', it shimmers in the light and is thought to be the luckiest of all crystals. Also called the Stone of Opportunity, use its winning, positive energy when you are after a boost in your fortunes or need a step-up in your career.

Malachite: a stone of transformation and protection.
This opaque, verdant crystal is often shot through with threads of white and represents the deep healing power of nature. It is a transformative stone that will help you grow spiritually and in your daily life. It is also a stone of protection: once thought to keep lightning and disease at bay. Tucked under a pillow, it can ease insomnia and avert depression. In Ancient Egypt, green was associated with death and resurrection. The afterlife was referred to as the Field of Malachite: a place without pain or suffering. A large polished piece of malachite can be costly, but you can pick up a tumbled stone cheaply.

Sapphire: azure serenity and wisdom.
The finest examples of this precious gemstone are a deep azure, the colour of the summer sky just before nightfall. Beautiful and translucent, it has long been held sacred in many religions: Hindus considered it one of the 'great gems' and used it as a temple offering and in astrology; the Ancient Greeks wore it when seeking answers from the Oracle at Delphi; and in Hebrew Lore, King Solomon and Abraham wore talismans of sapphire. It has not lost its power to activate psychic powers. Known as the Wisdom Stone, it also brings peace of mind and serenity of spirit.

HOW TO WORK WITH CRYSTALS

Choose a crystal that will help with what you need, then wear it as jewellery, carry it with you or work with it as follows.

- Place a crystal that suits the time of year on your altar, and work with its energies.

- During meditation, hold it in one or both hands, or place it in front of you on the floor. Use its energy to guide your meditation and to bring you back to centre if your mind wanders.

- Include a crystal in a ritual or spell, placing it in your magic circle (see *Summer Solstice: The Magic Circle*).

- Work with several crystals on a crystal grid (see *Crystals for Samhain: Design a crystal grid*), bringing awareness to how they respond to each other.

BELTANE TRADITIONS AND CUSTOMS

The joyful arrival of spring is at the heart of Beltane traditions. The revival in old pagan customs over recent years has seen maypoles erected once more at the heart of communities, while people with green faces parade through town as part of rollicking and joyful festivals.

The maypole

The maypole has long been central to pagan celebrations at Beltane and symbolizes the joy of new life returning. Traditionally, a tree was carefully chosen for its associations with fertility – oak, ash, birch, elm or fir, for example – then chopped down and all its branches removed. This pole was then decorated with long ribbons and festooned with flowers and erected in the centre of the village. Young people, alternating men and women ideally, held a ribbon each and danced around the pole, weaving in and out of each other in opposite directions until the ribbons were braided. The pole was left standing, to be burned at the end of the year as part of Samhain rituals.

Witch way: while most of us do not live in villages or have access to woodland to find our own tree, we can create mini maypoles to place on our altars or use as a table decoration. You will need a piece of dowel or a straight stick and 10 spools of brightly coloured ribbon. Cut the ribbons to size and stitch the ends together so that they radiate like spokes of a wheel. Attach the stitched ends to the top of the stick with glue. Decorate the top with flowers and leaves.

You could also make a stand for your maypole by drilling a hole in a piece of wood and inserting the pole, then gluing it in place.

The Green Man

On Beltane in certain British towns and villages (Hastings in Sussex and Clun in Shropshire are two examples), the streets are filled with green-faced people dancing and merrymaking, their heads and clothes covered with foliage. These are Green Man festivals, where a figure called Jack in the Green (also known as the Green Man or Green George) is paraded through town to give birth to the spirit of summer. The Green Man is the embodiment of the spirit of the forest and plants: he is the one who keeps the land green and lush to feed the cattle by making rain fall. In some festivals, he is dunked in a river or pond to ensure that enough rain will come. He appears all over Western Europe, as well as in parts of Asia and North Africa. You can spot him carved in stone at the tops of columns and above the doors of 12th to 16th century UK churches, peering through a mask of oak leaves, sometimes with horns. He is a powerful symbol at this time of year and well worth including in your Beltane magic.

BELTANE RITUALS AND SPELLS

Fire is at the heart of Beltane, so use it whenever you can. This could be as easy as lighting an extra candle on your altar, to something more extravagant like inviting friends over to dance around a bonfire. Beltane is also a time that honours the union of the female and the male, so it is a fitting time to balance those aspects in your life.

A solo ritual to attract love

If you are single and do not want to be, Beltane – the sabbat of fertility and sexuality – is a good time to find love. This ritual will help you along the way. Do it on a Friday, the day ruled by Venus – the planet of love and wisdom – preferably during the new moon phase for added oomph.

Find a quiet place where you will not be disturbed. Carve your initials into a pink candle with a knitting needle or penknife, and place the candle on your altar. Add anything else that you think may help your love ritual: crystals, flowers, a heart-shaped pebble...

On a piece of paper, draw a heart shape. How big it is, or what colour, is for you to decide. Make it represent how you are currently feeling: it could be small and blue if you are sad, for example, or big and red if you are feeling warm and happy. On another piece of paper, write down all the qualities you are looking for in a partner. Include their age, that they are available, and that they too are looking for a committed relationship.

Place your list and drawing on your altar and say: "Draw to me my perfect mate, that I may love dear and true. So mote it be." Repeat this at least three times while you gaze into the candle flame. See if an image of your future partner appears in your mind's eye. Thank the universe for helping you on your search, then ceremonially burn the two pieces of paper.

A BELTANE LOVE SACHET

WHAT YOU NEED

- a pinch each of: dried meadowsweet, dried ginger, dragon's blood resin, apple blossom, jasmine flowers, dried lavender and rose petals

- patchouli oil

- sandalwood oil

- a small fabric sachet or jar

- a piece of rose quartz

Put the dried ingredients into a small fabric sachet or a small jar, and add six drops each of the patchouli and sandalwood oil. Drop in the rose quartz. Place the sachet on your altar on a Friday night during a new moon and leave there for three days. After this time, carry the sachet in your handbag until your new love arrives.

A simple Beltane ritual with your witchy crew

This ritual works best with at least five people, including yourself, but you can adapt it if there are fewer of you.

Gather outside in a quiet place where you will not be disturbed, or set the scene at home by adding fresh spring flowers to your altar and spreading more flowers around the room. Fill a cauldron with kindling. After cleansing the space (see overleaf: *How to use your smudge stick*) gather your friends together in a circle.

Cast the circle (see *Summer Solstice: The Magic Circle*), then all say: "We give our energy to this circle, mingling with the spirits of nature to create a place of sanctuary, trust and peace. We have come here to celebrate Beltane and the abundance and fertility all around us. The Dark Time has ended and we are back once more in the light."

You light the kindling in the cauldron and say: "I kindle this fire to be a symbol of magic, to be a symbol of inspiration, to welcome the spirits into our magic circle."

You say: "Let us light the Beltane fire and dance in its light."

You stay by the altar as everyone else dances around the cauldron, jumping over it if there is room and it is safe.

As they dance, you say: "The year is a mighty wheel, and the sabbats are its spokes. This circle is also a wheel made up of witchy folks. Ahead now lies the sun, and around us spring is growing, with bud and twig and tree, we welcome Beltane merrily."

When the dancing ends, you say: "The celebration ends in peace as it began. May the blessings we have received nourish, strengthen and sustain us until we meet again. So mote it be!"

Everyone says: "So mote it be."

Unwind the circle and keep dancing!

WITCHY CRAFT

MAKE A SMUDGE STICK

Using herbs — sage in particular — to cleanse a space, or to heal and bless a person, has been practised in many cultures for centuries. Latterly, it has become associated with the indigenous peoples of the Americas, who set fire to white sage (*Salvia apiana*) and use its smoke in rituals and ceremonies.

Burning sage, tied into a bundle called a 'smudge stick', is a useful tool for the modern witch. White sage grows in southwestern USA and is not readily available in the UK, but common sage (*Salvia officinalis*) will work, too. A smudge stick is used to prepare a space before a ritual or performing a spell – the smoke 'washes off' the outside world and cleanses the area. It can also be used to bless or cleanse a person taking part in the ritual.

Herbs other than sage can also be used (see *Smudging herbs*, opposite), either on their own or in a bundle with other herbs. If you have your own herb garden or a few potted herbs, now is the best time to harvest them to make a smudge stick as the new growth has just appeared and is fresh and vital. Choose the time of collection carefully: you may want to pick your herbs at full moon for maximum effect, for example.

WHAT YOU NEED

- a handful of dried sage twigs with leaves, cut into manageable lengths of around 10cm. Alternatively, select another herb of your choosing, or a mixture of several. (See box, opposite for some suggestions.) Dried flowers can also be used: rosebuds would add another layer of fragrance. Before choosing your herb, think of how you will use the smudge stick and which is most useful for that purpose.

- twine

- flowers, to decorate

- a fireproof bowl or large shell, to capture falling ash

- a bird's feather, to fan the smoke

How to use your smudge stick

Open the doors and windows of the space you are clearing so that unwanted energy can escape. Light the smudge stick, allowing it to catch fire. After about 20 seconds, blow the flames out and let the smoke billow around. Use a feather to waft the smoke around the space or over the person or object that is being cleansed. Extinguish the smudge stick by stubbing it out in a fireproof bowl.

Making the smudge stick

Here is how to put everything together.

① Gather your herbs together so that they form a neat bundle.

② Trim the ends neatly and tie tightly with twine so that the bundle is secure.

③ Wrap the entire bundle with twine, adding and binding in additional herbs and flowers for a fatter or more decorative finish. Leave until the herbs are completely dry and your smudge stick is ready to burn.

Smudging herbs

Include one or several of these in your smudge bundle.

Sage: has been used by countless cultures to disperse negativity, bless, cleanse and heal. There are several types of sage: Californian white sage (*salvia apiana*) is considered the best, but garden sage (*salvia officinalis*) will suit our purposes if you cannot get white sage.

Cedar: burning a piece of cedar is one way to cleanse a home when first moving in, and to invite unwanted spirits to leave. Cedar helps protect a person, place or object from unwanted influences.

Juniper: boosts mental and physical energy levels.

Rosemary: a purifying cleanser. Effective if added to a bundle of sage.

Palo Santo: use this South American wood, known by shaman as 'holy wood', as the core of your smudge stick, then pack sage around it. It is a powerful energy cleanser.

Lavender: invites friendly spirits into your sacred space. You can also smudge it over your bed to rid it of unwanted energy to help you sleep.

Basil: include some basil in your smudge stick if you want to attract love.

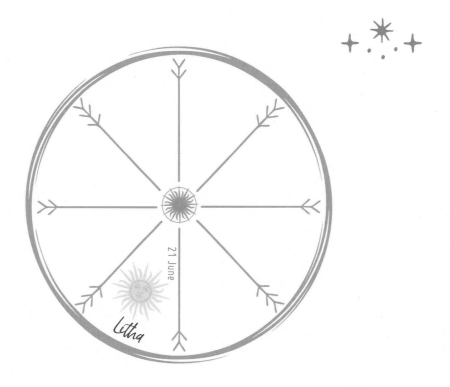

21 June

Litha

Litha, Sabbat of the Summer Solstice: 21 June*

Summer solstice: the longest day. A time of intense, active energy and powerful magic.

There is magic, and a little madness, in the air on the eve of the summer solstice. Witches and fairies roam about, spreading mischief and mayhem. The Earth vibrates with energy and abundance. It is a time of joyful celebration, a chance to escape the everyday, to stay out all night and relish the moment.

The summer solstice occurs when the North Pole is angled towards the sun more than on any other day of the year. This results in the longest period of sunlight for the Northern Hemisphere*. For a brief moment, the sun appears to hang stationary in the sky. (The word 'solstice' is from the Latin *sol* meaning 'sun' and *stitium* – 'still' or 'stopped'). It is a day of endless possibilities and promise and a time of fulfilment. Seeds planted in spring come into flower now, and plans made earlier in the year begin to flourish.

Traditionally, the summer solstice was celebrated with fire to honour the fullness of the sun and to boost its strength. Bonfires were lit on hill tops, burning wheels were rolled down mountains and lovers jumped over flames. A summer solstice bonfire is a joyful thing and a good way to gather your witchy friends together and watch the flames flicker as the light slowly fades.

This is a very energetic and positive time for all types of spells and magic, so it's important to make the most of it. The sun is associated with masculine energy, so harness it to bring out your inner power and strength. Use herbs picked at midnight on Midsummer's Eve (the night before the solstice) in spells to attract love and money: they will be especially potent now. Seize the moment and embrace the magic because it will not last. Hanging over this powerful, sun-filled day is a lengthening shadow. From now on, the days will gradually become shorter, the nights longer and we will slip back into the dark.

* In the Northern Hemisphere, the summer solstice falls on or around 21 June. If you are in the Southern Hemisphere, i.e. below the equator, it will be on or around 21 December.

On your summer solstice altar

Celebrate the warmth and light of the sun and the abundance it brings with a vase of flowers on your altar. Add a pot of honey and scatter around rose petals and oak leaves. Light white candles to represent solar power, then add crystals and a symbol of the sun – draw or model one if you do not have one ready made.

THE MAGIC CIRCLE

Circles have had a magical significance since ancient times, and they are at the heart of the modern witch's work. All ceremonies, spells and rituals take place within a circle which, after casting (see overleaf), becomes a sacred and purified space. The circle encloses the witch and is a boundary that concentrates the power and the magic within it. The Wheel of Life – which, as we have seen, governs the witch's year – is also circular and reminds us of the life-death-life cycle.

The circle's simple, perfect and eternal geometry is rich with symbolism. It is a shape without beginning or end, without sides and without corners. As such it represents eternity, wholeness and infinity and has played a vital role in many different cultures for millennia. The Ancient Chinese yin yang (*taijitu*) symbol is a circle split into two opposite parts; another symbol known as the ouroboros, which originated in Ancient Egypt but has been adopted by other magical traditions, is a circular snake eating its own tail; and the medicine wheel, or sacred hoop, has been used by generations of Native American people for health and healing. In astrology, a circle is the symbol of the moon; the symbol for the sun is a circle with a dot at its centre. Circles are seen everywhere in nature, from the shape of the Earth itself, to birds' nests, flowers and the rings of a tree.

OUROBOROS

THE EARTH

YIN YANG

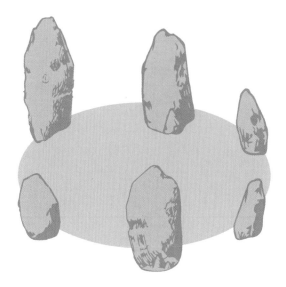

Stone circles and the solstice

The power of the circle was recognized by our ancestors who built massive circular stone temples. Ancient, awesome and sacred, stone circles and other megaliths are scattered across landscapes worldwide. These precise astronomical clocks followed the movement of the sun, moon and stars. It is also likely that they were intended as solar temples* where rituals and ceremonies that honoured the heavens and its deities were performed

Built to align with the sun's movements during the solstices, stones were hauled into place and erected vertically to frame the sunrise for those standing at particular points.

Archaeologists claim that the most famous of all stone circles, Stonehenge, was built to point exactly to the midsummer sunrise. The sun rises behind the Heel Stone in the north-east, and its rays shine into the heart of the circle. The size and scale of the circle indicate that significant gatherings once took place here. This is also true in modern times as large numbers of people turn up at Stonehenge and other circles to celebrate the sun coming up at the summer solstice. According to legend, other stones, such as those at Coetan Arthur in Wales, uproot themselves and walk around.

Witch way: while larger gatherings at the summer solstice can be celebratory and uplifting, a smaller or solitary ceremony can offer a deeper connection with the stones, the ancestors who erected them and the solstice itself. The adventurous witch could locate a less-visited ancient circle or megalith and spend the summer solstice there, quietly waiting for the sun to come up, then honouring it with spells, offerings and incantations.

* Others, such as Callanish in the Outer Hebrides, Scotland, were built to align with the movement of the moon.

CASTING A CIRCLE

Before undertaking any spell or ritual, it is important to surround yourself and any other witches who are with you with a protective circle. This will prevent unfriendly spirits and negative energy coming near and will keep you safe.

HOW TO CAST A CIRCLE

Gather all the things you will need – your cauldron, athame, besom, herbs, crystals, incense and candles – and place them at your feet. They must be inside the circle throughout.

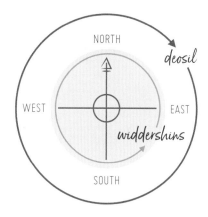

Trace the circle with your athame or wand (see *What a Witch Needs*) or walk around it *deosil* (in a clockwise direction). Customarily, witches' circles are 9ft (2.7m) in diameter, although this can vary depending on the number of people within it. You could use a cord or length of thick string to mark the outline of the circle.

Invite any others in through a 'gate' in the circle cut with your athame, then shut it behind them. Light a candle at each of the four cardinal points, or quarters, of the circle.

Face east, where the sun and moon rise. Think of the element of air. Imagine it flowing through you, then radiating out into the world. Say: "Blessings to the east and all those who live there."

Turn to face south. Think of the element of fire. Imagine its warmth pulsing from the core of your body, then radiating out into the world. Say: "Blessings to the south and all those who live there."

Now face west. Think of the element of water. Imagine it showering over you in a soft, purifying spray, then spreading out into the world. Say: "Blessings to the west and all those who live there."

Finally face north. Think of the element of earth. Feel your feet on the ground and imagine a beam of green light shining down through the top of your head, into your body and out through the soles of your feet into the earth. Say: "Blessings to the north and all those who live there. The circle is cast."

Rid the circle of any negative energy by symbolically brushing it out with your besom. Invite any deities or spirits to join you, then state the purpose of what you are about to undertake, for example, a sabbat ritual or a spell.

Now work your magic! When you have finished, thank the spirits and any deities you have invited, then blow out the candles. Unwind the circle by either tracing it or walking around its circumference *widdershins* (in an anti-clockwise direction).

SUMMER PLANTS FOR REMEDIES AND SPELLS

Midsummer, with its combination of maximum sunlight and warm temperatures, sees certain plants at their absolute best. These are the ones said to have greater potency now than at other times, which is increased if the herbs are gathered on the day of the summer solstice and used immediately in spells.

Rue (*Ruta graveolens):* The pretty yellow flowers of this ancient herb rise above its feathery blue-green foliage at midsummer. It was once widely used medicinally and in cooking but has fallen out of favour in modern times. This is probably because it has a bitter taste, smells disagreeable and can irritate the skin and the digestion. Best, then, not to ingest it fresh but use it dried. Traditionally, it was added to incense and worn around the neck to prevent ill health. The Romans carried it to keep away the evil eye, as a protection against poison and to keep werewolves at bay. While none of these things trouble us much these days, it can still be sprinkled on the floor or hung by the door to banish negativity.

Vervain (*Verbena officinalis):* This elegant plant with long stems and pretty purple flowers is also known as The Witch's Herb and The Herb of Enchantment. It's best gathered at midsummer when it is in full flower and at maximum strength. Vervain has been held sacred by witches, priests and magicians for centuries – it was the sacred herb of the Goddess Isis – and has many magical uses. Wearing a crown of Vervain is said to protect you when casting a spell; an infusion sprinkled around the home chases away unpleasant atmospheres; and it is a common ingredient in love potions, and prosperity and protective spells. It is even said to be the vampire's greatest weakness: any physical contact with it will burn them.

Bay (*Laurus nobilis):* This evergreen, aromatic shrub is easy to grow. Planted in a sunny spot in the garden or in a pot, it will produce plenty of shiny leaves for the modern witch to add to potions and spells. Associated with the sun and the element of fire, it's time for magic is now. It brings prosperity and luck, so use it in spells that attract either. It is also said to encourage psychic visions – Greek priestesses of Apollo chewed its leaves and inhaled the fumes of dried leaves to help with divination. Add to a sage smudge stick to waft its healing and purifying smoke around the house or to cleanse a space before a ritual.

St. John's Wort (*Hypericum*): Although it flowers for most of the summer, St. John's Wort is at its most powerful now. (It is named after St. John the Baptist: the Christian festival of St. John's Day coincides with the summer solstice.) Its yellow, five-petalled flowers with their sunburst of stamens are a cheerful addition to the garden. This is a kindly plant that makes good things happen. It has been used for divination and to ease hallucinations, and it continues to be used in tablet form as a mild antidepressant. It is also said to have magical properties if you are looking for a mate: collect a sprig wet with dew on St. John's Day and you will be wed within a year.

Witch ways: Harness the power of these seasonal plants in the following ways. See *A Witch's Herbal* for directions on making infusions.

- Mix an infusion of rue with morning dew and sprinkle around your circle before performing magical acts to give you protection and banish negativity.

- Include stems of vervain in a bridal bouquet: not only will it look pretty, but it will keep love alive between the couple getting married.

- Write a wish on a bay leaf in gold ink. Hold it over your cauldron and burn with a candle to make your wish come true.

- Make a St. John's Wort skin balm. On a dry, sunny day, pick enough flowers of St. John's Wort to fill a jam jar. Fill the jar with olive oil, making sure the flowers are covered. Put the lid on and place on a sunny windowsill. The oil will gradually turn red. After a month or so, strain and remove the flowers. The oil is ready to use.

ST. JOHN'S WORT

CRYSTALS FOR THE SUMMER SOLSTICE

We know that crystals naturally attract positive energy and help to manifest intentions, but at midsummer, they get an extra charge. These crystals, which all embody the fiery strength of the sun and glow with its warm and powerful radiance, will act like a catalyst on spells and give a boost to your desires and intentions. These feel powerful now:

Tiger's Eye: lustrous stone to instil courage. This mysterious and powerful stone glows with layers of lustrous gold, tawny brown and black. When polished and cut into a sphere you can see how it gets its name: it almost flickers like the eye of a tiger. The Ancient Egyptians used it for the eyes in their statues of gods to express divine vision. Believed to provide the protection of the sun, it instils courage and nourishes the soul. Used in meditation, it will ground you with its warm and stable energy. Placed on an altar or on a grid, it will attract luck and good fortune; not in one dramatic burst, but in a steady and consistent flow.

Amber: bright healing energy like sunlight captured. Transparent and golden, amber resembles solidified honey or captured sunlight. It is not a stone, but fossilized resin that once bubbled from ancient trees. Young amber is less than 100,000 years old, but older stones can date back millions of years. The older the amber, the more valuable it is. Associated with the sun, it emits a bright, healing energy and has accumulated mystical properties. In Asian cultures, it is thought to be the soul of the tiger and is carried for protection on long and potentially hazardous journeys. Think of it as a warm, wise and protective friend that can help you along your witch's journey.

Golden Calcite: uplifting energy to brighten the mind. Pale yellow, transparent, and glowing with an inner light, golden calcite is like a hardened drop of sunshine. Found in abundance, especially in Mexico, it is an affordable and effective stone that brings an uplifting energy to your witchy practice. It can brighten the mind, dispel gloom and banish stagnant energy. It is a clean, clear, bright presence on a crystal grid.

Sunstone: the power of the sun in a blood-red stone. Rose-coloured and speckled with shimmering red particles, sunstone embodies the power of the sun. One legend of the indigenous people of North America suggests that it is the blood of a powerful warrior who was wounded by an arrow in a skirmish. It is an important stone for matters of the heart and aligns body and spirit.

A MANIFESTATION RITUAL
FOR THE SUMMER SOLSTICE

First, think about what is missing in your life right now. Choose the most important thing so as not to over-complicate matters.

Now select a a crystal that feels right for the summer solstice. Light a candle. Write your intention on a piece of paper. Hold your crystal in your non-dominant hand (the left hand if you are right handed, and vice versa). Breathe deeply. As you exhale think about what the manifestation of your intention looks like and how it will make you feel.

SUMMER SOLSTICE TRADITIONS AND CUSTOMS

The summer solstice or midsummer, also known as Litha, is one of most important and widespread solar festivals in Europe and throughout the world. It has been celebrated worldwide for centuries but reached its peak during the Middle Ages, when the streets were ablaze with midsummer bonfires.

Bonfires

Celtic people stayed up all night on Midsummer's Eve to welcome the sun and watch it rise. As darkness fell, the land was sprinkled with flames: fires were lit on top of hills to boost the sun's strength and to ensure a healthy harvest. Bonfires were set alight at holy wells and other sacred places; torches were carried sunwise (in the direction of the sun's apparent movement across the sky) around homes and fields for good luck; and cattle were blessed by leading them through low-lying flames. People jumped over fires to keep demons away, and lovers leapt hand in hand through the flames to bless their relationship. The coals from these fires were then scattered on the fields to encourage a good harvest. Bonfires were also thought to be medicinal and purify the air.

Decorations and processions

Houses and churches were decorated with wreaths made from birch twigs, fennel, St. John's Wort and other summertime greenery. In late Medieval England, large and noisy processions run by trade guilds with giants, devils, hobby horses, drummers, trumpeters and tableaux depicting famous scenes paraded through town.

Love divinations

During the Middle Ages, midsummer was customarily the time when girls would try to discover who they would marry. One method was to throw hemp seed over their shoulders outdoors at night. Their future husband would then appear. Another was to slip two stems of orpine (a purple-flowered sedum) into the joists of the house. One represented the man; the other his sweetheart. If one stem bent towards the other then marriage was on the cards, if it went the other way, then it was not. If either stem withered, then death would follow.

Witch way: a simple spell to show the universe that you are open to love is to head to the sea, a river or a stream. Take a handful of rose petals with you. Visualize the person you would like to meet, then throw the petals into the water. As you throw them, say the following incantation nine times: "Away with solitude, I will no more be alone. As the petals move into the sea, so true love will come to me."

SOLSTICE WREATH

SUMMER SOLSTICE RITUALS AND SPELLS

The best way to honour midsummer is to get outdoors. A simple act like swimming in a sparkling river, climbing the boughs of an ancient tree or walking in a meadow can bring its own powerful magic. Now is also a time to celebrate with friends. Gather around a bonfire, eat outdoors, lie in the sun and be grateful for what this time of year brings.

Simple solo summer meditation

On a sunny day, go outside and find somewhere quiet where you will not be disturbed. Close your eyes and feel the warmth of the sun on your face and body. Breathe steadily and deeply. Imagine the sun entering your body from the top of your head, then coursing down through your throat, arms, chest and legs. Picture yourself filled with light, then imagine this light radiating from your solar plexus (the centre of your chest between the naval and breasts), bathing everything around you with light and love. Sit in the peace and calm of the power of the sun until it feels right to move. Imagine the light draining from your body through the soles of your feet. Thank the sun for the meditation.

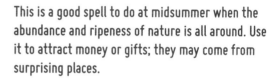

SUMMER SOLSTICE SPELL
TO BRING PROSPERITY

This is a good spell to do at midsummer when the abundance and ripeness of nature is all around. Use it to attract money or gifts; they may come from surprising places.

WHAT YOU NEED

- a green candle
- dried sage leaves
- a cauldron

Witch way: with the point of a sharp knife or a knitting needle, inscribe your name into the candle. Carve something that represents money: a pound sign should do it. Light the candle and place it in the cauldron. Sprinkle the candle with the sage leaves. As the candle burns down, imagine what it will feel like to receive the money and what good you will do with it. Say aloud: "By the power of the sun, bring now to me wealth and prosperity. Bring it to me with harm to none. So mote it be." Let the candle burn itself out.

A summer solstice ritual with your witchy crew

Cast your circle (see *Summer Solstice: The Magic Circle*). In its centre, place a cut-out symbol that represents the sun - a simple circle or something more complex. Invite your friends into the circle.

You say: "The sun is high in the sky. With hope in our hearts, let us spread happiness about us."

Everyone turns to the south.

You say: "Let us walk away from everything that irks or damages us."

Each person writes down what they want to let go of and leaves their note in the north quadrant of the circle.

Everyone faces north.

You say: "Let us invite friendships and alliances into our lives that will enrich them and help us to grow."

Each person writes down who they would like to invite into their lives and leaves the note in the south quadrant.

Everyone faces west.

You say: "Let us walk away from negativity, meanness, unpleasantness and ill humour."

Each person writes down the characteristics they wish to banish from their behaviour and leaves the note in the west quadrant.

Everyone faces east.

You say: "Let us develop positivity and learning so that we continue to grow in the second half of the year."

Each person writes down what they would like to learn and manifest during the rest of the year.

Once all quadrants have been addressed, light the candles: north first, then south, west and finally east.

You say: "Power of the sun we now are one, shine forth all that is to come, release all that is done, now bring in the fun, for everyone."

Everyone says: "So mote it be."

Celebrate with feasting and dancing, preferably wildly, around a bonfire!

WITCHY CRAFT

MAKE A FLORAL CROWN

If anyone knows how to do midsummer, it's the Swedes. After winters with very little daylight, the endless summer days are celebrated on 24 June, with Midsommarstång.

Festivities include erecting maypoles (called Midsommarstången), which is thought to link the underworld with the earth and the sky. This belief is linked to the Old Norse Tree of Life, Yggdrasill, which connected all three. There is also feasting on herring and strawberries, drinking of schnapps, and frog dancing where everyone, whatever their age, hops around the maypole singing a song about frogs.

All of this is done wearing a floral* crown. This most seasonal and attractive headgear is easy to make and just the thing for your own solstice ritual. Make it the day before the summer solstice and wear it as the sun comes up and all day long.

WHAT YOU NEED

- florist's wire
- florist's tape
- florist's copper wire
- flowers and foliage: choose a good mix of leaves like eucalyptus or asparagus fern and add whatever flowers are blooming or that you can find easily. Roses, nigella, carnations, dianthus and campanula all work well.

* Another Swedish midsummer tradition is to pick seven different species of flower from seven different places and put all of them under your pillow. Fall asleep and you will dream of your future partner.

Making the crown

Before you begin, put the flowers and foliage in a bucket of water for an hour or so to give them a good drink. This prevents them from wilting prematurely.

(1) Trim the foliage into manageable pieces and snip the flower stems so that they are small and easier to fasten.

(2) Make a circle with the florist's wire and fit it to your head. Double it with another round of wire, then cover both with florist's tape so it looks neat and there are no snagging ends.

(3) Attach the end of a spool of florist's copper wire to your circle, and attach the foliage piece by piece, overlapping as you go.

(4) Add the flower sprigs following the same method.

(5) When your crown looks full and lovely, tie the end of the copper wire to the circle to keep it secure. Cover the end with florist's tape.

(6) Now put it on and admire your handiwork! Spritz the crown with water every so often to keep it fresh.

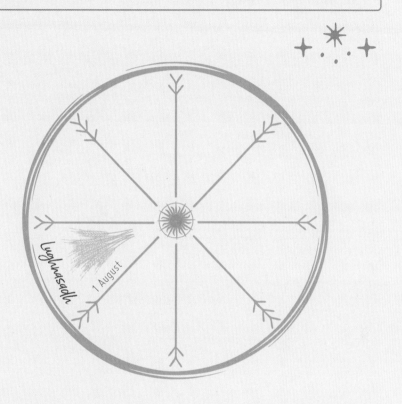

Sabbat of Lughnasadh:
1 August*

Lughnasadh: the first harvest. Plants are fruiting. A time to be grateful for what has been created.

The wheel of the year turns towards autumn. The days are shortening and there is a suggestion of the coming shadow days hanging in the air. Jumpers are pulled on in the evenings and vegetables are dug up and enjoyed. Summer's growth has ended and the first harvest has begun. For the agricultural worker, this is the time when cereal crops are cut down, bundled up and milled for flour. The first apples, pears and soft fruits are ready to pick. There is an abundance everywhere.

The origins of Lughnasadh* lie in pagan Ireland: the word derives from *Lugh*, a Celtic god of grain, craftsmanship and the sun, and *nasadh,* meaning 'assembly' or 'commemoration'. Great gatherings that lasted several weeks were held to honour Lugh, including athletic games and copious amounts of feasting. Many of these took place on top of mountains and hills and included customs, such as the 'sacrifice' of a corn figure to ensure the fertility of next year's crops.

The festival was adopted by Christians and called Lammas (from the Old English *hlafmasse,* means 'loaf mass'). It continued to be a time of feasting, fairs and general revelries. People still climb mountains on the last Sunday of July, most notably Reek Sunday, a pilgrimage to the top of Croagh Patrick in Ireland.

For the modern witch, Lughnasadh is a chance to stop and take stock. Those spiritual and emotional seeds sown earlier in the year are ready to be harvested. How have they grown? Have you neglected your dreams and ambitions? Day-to-day stuff can get in the way and make you forget about where you should be heading. Rekindle the magic of your hopes by spending time now listening to your heart, not your head. The power of meditation, rituals and spells will help you manifest what you really want and need.

* In the Northern Hemisphere, Lughnasadh falls on or around 1 August. If you are in the Southern Hemisphere, it will be on or around 1 February.

On your Lughnasadh altar

Lughnasadh is about gratitude for the first harvest and the food that nature provides. Echo this by adding stalks of corn, wheat or barley to your altar if you can find them, or use a small loaf of bread if you cannot. Add yellow and green candles to represent the harvest and the sun, a corn dolly (see *Witchy Craft* later in this chapter) and a bunch of meadowsweet or other summer flowers. If you have a pendulum, put it on the altar with your crystals to be blessed.

PENDULUM POWER

Every witch should have her own pendulum. This simplest of devices – a piece of crystal, metal or wood hanging from a chain – is a key to a world of wonder. It can unlock magic, reveal energy paths, answer troubling questions and help you understand yourself and the world around you better. A pendulum is also a lovely thing and can be carried around easily in a pocket or a bag, to be produced whenever it is needed.

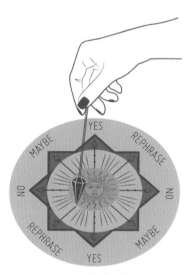

Dowsing

The method by which pendulums reveal their magic is called 'dowsing'. Dowsing is associated in many people's minds with searching for water. The traditional method of doing this is with a Y-shaped piece of wood or two rods of L-shaped metal, but a pendulum will work, too. A pendulum is also used by dowsers to trace ley lines – energy paths that connect landmarks in the landscape: a fascinating subject in itself (see overleaf: *Leylines: cosmic energy pathways*).

Most witches, however, use their pendulums to clarify puzzling messages they have received, or to guide them towards a decision. The movement of the pendulum, which can either be a rotation or a swing back and forth, supplies a simple 'yes' or 'no' answer to any query. It is a straightforward, visual representation of the subtle energies at play around us. The answer to a carefully considered question could come from your own intuition or from your spirit guides.

On a more mundane level, a pendulum can help you find things that are lost or indicate whether food is good for you. One old custom was to hold a wedding ring on a piece of string over a pregnant woman's belly. If it swung to the left, she would have a boy; to the right, a girl.

YES/NO CHART

How to make a pendulum

There are no rules when it comes to making a pendulum. Anything that feels comfortable and can swing freely works well. You could use a crystal pendant, or make one from wood, a shell or a metal charm. Use something that you feel a connection with for the best results. Attach it to a piece of string or a chain and you are ready to go.

HOW TO USE YOUR PENDULUM

Before and after use, purify your pendulum by washing it in saltwater or passing it through burning sage or incense.

Find a quiet place and concentrate on being still. Relax your wrist and hold the pendulum between your thumb and index finger, letting it dangle.

Think carefully about what question you will ask; keep it simple: it has to be one that can only be answered with a yes, no or maybe. Work out which way the pendulum swings or rotates for 'yes' and which for 'no' by asking it a straightforward question first, e.g. "Are my eyes blue?" or "Do I live in this house?". Do the same for 'maybe'.

Consider who will guide you to the answer for your question: it could be a goddess, a spirit guide, the universe or your own intuition.

Ask your question and allow the pendulum to swing freely until it settles in one strong direction and provides your answer. This may not happen immediately, but be patient, it will!

Pendulum charts

Once you have got the hang of working with a pendulum, you can expand its power beyond answering simple yes or no questions with a pendulum chart. There are many types of these, some more complicated than others. Most are semi-circular, but some more elaborate versions are full circles.

You can buy a ready-made chart or draw one yourself; it need not be complicated. Keep it simple to begin with: draw a semi-circle and write the letters of the alphabet at regular intervals around its edge. Draw another, smaller semi-circle inside and write numbers from 0–10 around that. Mark a point at the centre of the base of the semi-circle. This is where you hold the pendulum.

Now think of your question. Make sure it is phrased carefully and that you are ready for a truthful response. Write the question on a piece of paper and place it beside the chart. Centre yourself and connect with whatever guides you, then place the pendulum over the point you have marked and ask your question out loud. Be patient and the pendulum will swing to the section of the chart that will answer your question. Do not forget to thank your guides for their help.

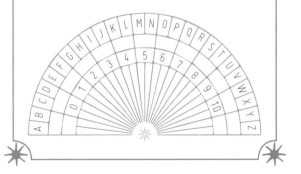

Leylines: cosmic energy pathways

Leylines are invisible tracks linking ancient and sacred sites and geographical features. They were first noticed by a man called Alfred Watkins in 1921 on a country road in Herefordshire. He noticed that a series of landmarks and other features lined up, "like a chain of fairy lights". These lines, which criss-crossed the country, he suggested, could have been ceremonial pathways or routes used by traders. In more recent times, the theory of leylines was rekindled with ley hunters searching for lines of energy or cosmic alignments. Because they cannot be seen, one way to find them is with a pendulum. Take yours to a sacred site such as a stone circle, churchyard or holy well. As you walk around, dangle the pendulum and notice when it swings. You could be tracking the course of a leyline.

KNOW YOUR TALISMANS, AMULETS AND CHARMS

Beyond your pendulum, various other magical objects can be
helpful to the modern witch and are used in rituals and spells
to channel supernatural powers.

POCKET TALISMAN

HAND OF FATIMA

FOUR-LEAVED CLOVER

Talismans: these are used for a particular purpose such as finding success at work or attracting love, and usually last for a limited time. Once the goal has been achieved, the talisman should be buried or thrown into a body of water. Inscribed with a variety of symbols (a pentagram or an ankh is common), numbers and astrological signs, and combinations of all of these, it is made by someone who knows what they are doing and is often used in ritual magic.

Amulets: these are worn or carried to keep harm away and protect you from evil. Unlike a talisman, which lasts for a specific length of time, an amulet goes on forever. The Hand of Fatima and the Evil Eye are good examples of amulets.

Charms: A lucky charm is thought to bring good fortune. They come in all sorts of shapes and sizes, from a horseshoe to a four-leaved clover. Some are blessed or infused with powers from a sacred place, for example, using water taken from a holy well and poured into a container.

LUGHNASADH PLANTS FOR REMEDIES AND SPELLS

The sunny, hazy days of August are filled with the scent and blossom of wildflowers. Scattered through meadows and springing up alongside the road, several of them are especially useful in the modern witch's herb cupboard.

Lavender *(Lavandula):* The heady scent of lavender is one of the most recognisable smells of summer. The tiny purple flower clusters at the top of long stems shoot out from silvery green foliage, filling the air with a heavenly scent. As well as smelling so good, lavender has numerous healing and spell-craft uses. It is a vital ingredient in love spells and sachets. You could also rub it on a love letter to attract a mate. A pouch packed with lavender under the pillow will ease you to sleep, as will burning the dried flowers in an incense mix. As an essential oil, lavender has powerful antiseptic properties and is used to help skin conditions. Queen Elizabeth I is said to have drunk lavender infusions to cure her migraines.

Meadowsweet *(Filipendula ulmaria):* The frothy blooms of this, the most summery of plants, line the hedgerows and riverbanks now, filling the air with its sweet, almond aroma. Bring it indoors to infuse your house with the heavenly scent. Meadowsweet's general loveliness has led to a romantic reputation: its other names are Bride of the Meadow and Lady of the Meadow. Use dried flowers in your spell and incense mixtures and place fresh blooms on your altar to attract love. Meadowsweet mead (a delicious drink made with honey and water) is also a rewarding thing to try, as is meadowsweet jelly and jam.

Yarrow *(Achillea millefolium):* With its feathery leaves and clusters of white flowers, yarrow is easy to spot in meadows and fields. If unsure, crush its leaves: they have a strong, aromatic scent. Yarrow has a long history as a remedy for various ailments, from staunching nosebleeds to lowering blood pressure, treating snakebites and as a chest rub for colds. As an infusion, it is even said to prevent (not cure!) baldness. Like mugwort, it was used by witches to increase their psychic power and to attract suitors. According to folklore, if you pin it to your clothing, stand next to the person you are attracted to, then put it in a drawer, the next day that person will reciprocate your love.

The witchiest plant of all: mandrake

The berries of the mandrake plant glow with an eerie phosphorescence at dawn. This is reason enough to make it seem magical, but its real power lies beneath the soil. The taproot of the mandrake looks spookily like a miniature person with gnarly arms and legs.

   Folklore has it that the plant screeches and sweats blood when pulled from the ground, and whoever digs it up will die in agony. While this is an appealing but fanciful notion, the plant is indeed poisonous (see *A word of warning* below) and difficult to propagate by division. Best to leave it alone and enjoy the superstitions and legends that surround it. In Greek mythology, for example, it was the plant of Circe, the witch goddess, who made a juice from it to turn Odysseus' men into pigs. And Medieval witches were said to harvest it at night beneath the gallows where it sprung up from beneath the bodies of dead men.

MANDRAKE

Witch ways: Here are some ways to capture the benefits of these seasonal plants. See *A Witch's Herbal* for directions on making infusions and drying herbs.

- A tea made from meadowsweet blossom soothes coughs and colds.

- Include yarrow in a bridal bouquet or hang over the marriage bed to ensure the couple stay happily married for at least seven years.

- In Elizabethan times, meadowsweet was 'strewn' (scattered) over the floor to freshen the room and because it made the "heart merrie and joyful and delighteth the senses".

- Cut long stems of lavender when it is at its best. Bundle together with string, then hang upside down until the flowers are dry. You can then use them in incense or spell work.

A word of warning: do not be tempted to eat mandrake root or include it any drinks. It is poisonous — ingestion can lead to vomiting, hallucinations, diarrhoea and even, in severe cases, to the slowing of the heartbeat and death.

LUGHNASADH ✧

CRYSTALS FOR LUGHNASADH

Late summer is all about appreciating the sun and the powerful benefits of the natural world. Choose crystals that harness solar energy and correspond with the rhythms of nature for maximum potency and results. These feel powerful now:

Peridot: a stone of late summer warmth.
The yellow/green colour of this translucent stone evokes late summer and the arrival of autumn. Associated with the sun, it is a cheerful crystal that beams warmth and wellbeing, valued for its powers to drive away darkness. Formed as molten rock ejected onto the Earth's surface by earthquakes and volcanoes, it represents coming out of the dark and into the light. Peridot is a powerful crystal used for energetic cleansing: use it to help banish negative emotions and behaviour, and to give your confidence a boost.

Sardonyx: a striped badge of courage.
The fiery reddish brown of this stone, also known as sard or carnelian, is shot through with paler bands of onyx, giving this crystal a richly striped appearance. This dual colour has been exploited by artists and sculptors over the centuries who have carved into it, revealing different bands of colour. The Romans crafted rings and amulets from it carved with an image of Mars, God of War, for protection and courage going into battle. It is a useful crystal to have around if feeling nervous or in need of a shot of bravery: it will calm and ground you while strengthening your purpose and willpower.

Golden topaz: a glamorous stone of generosity and joy.
This gorgeous crystal is known as the Crystal of the Sun, appropriate for this time of year when every sunny day is treasured. It has many different colour manifestations, from pure golden sun to fiery pink, each one radiating creativity and abundance. Its solar energy embodies joy and generosity. If you are feeling spiritually or physically depleted, golden topaz can recharge you. It will also help you manifest those desires that feel elusive and inspire your creativity. Good to have near you during meditation, it is like a ray of sunshine connecting you to the universe and the divine.

Moss agate: like a still, magical pool.
Looking into this mysterious stone is like looking into a still pool fronded with feathery plants. Translucent and milky white, moss agate gets its name from the green mossy filaments that run through it and look as though they are trapped in a bubble of water. Associated with nature spirits, this stone will help you tune into the energies of your garden, vegetable plot or houseplants. Moss agate is all about honouring Mother Earth, and rebuilding your connection with nature through growing, gardening, animals and a simple appreciation of the natural world. It can also be used in spells to attract abundance and prosperity.

SOLAR CHARGE

Make the most of the last summer days by charging your stones in the sunlight.

Witch way: Leave your crystal outside for a few hours only in a sunny spot. It will absorb the solar warmth and vitality and then gently radiate it throughout the colder, darker months.

LUGHNASADH TRADITIONS AND CUSTOMS

Nowadays, witches celebrate the eve of Lughnasadh on the 31 July and the sabbat on 1 August, but it was not always so. Festivities celebrating the first harvest and the god Lugh were known to have lasted for four weeks in pre-Christian Ireland. These were massive gatherings that included religious ceremonies, matchmaking and athletic contests.

These gatherings continued into modern times with annual fairs and 'wakes' taking place in agricultural communities. Farm workers attended wakes to mourn the death of the Corn King (also known as the Green Man – see *Beltane Traditions and Customs*), whose sacrifice through the harvest meant there would be bread through the winter months. These included funerary rites and processions followed by the celebration of a new king with games, feasting and magic.

Other Lughnasadh customs

- A brittle toffee called the Yellow Man is traditionally served at the Lammas Fair in County Antrim in Ireland.

- Bilberries are traditionally collected at this time: the Sunday nearest to Lughnasadh is sometimes called Bilberry Sunday. If there are plenty of bilberries, next year's harvest will be plentiful, too.

- Garlands of flowers are placed around holy wells, and 'clootie rags' are tied in nearby trees as offerings on Garland Sunday. Visitors pray for health and walk *deosil* (clockwise) around the well.

Handfasting

This rite of marriage was performed in pre-Christian Ireland at Lughnasadh. According to legend, Lughnasadh celebrates the marriage of Lugh to the goddess Eriu, a hag who turned into a beauty at the altar. Lughnasadh is also nine months from Beltane, the birth of summer and life.

Modern witches have revived the tradition of handfasting and often 'tie the knot' on 1 August, usually outdoors and always inside a magic circle of friends and family. The couple hold left hands, and a High Priest or Priestess binds their hands together with cord or ribbon. They then move around the circle, showing their bound hands and spreading their happiness and love. The High Priest or Priestess unties their bindings and declares them handfasted. In some ceremonies the couple then jump over a broomstick for good luck. Like conventional weddings, feasting and merriment follows, but unlike conventional weddings, handfasting is not a legal marriage ceremony.

LUGHNASADH RITUALS AND SPELLS

This time of year has a wistful quality as summer starts to fade and there is a hint of autumn in the air. Responding to the changing season can be as simple as putting your hands in the earth and thanking it for the harvest or waking early to greet the sun with an incantation. But Lughnasadh offers the opportunity to celebrate the bounty with feasts.

Simple solo spell: make a gratitude jar

Think about what you are grateful for. This does not need to relate to food, and could be your family or pets, or something as simple as a sunny morning or warm fire. Every day until the autumn equinox, write down one thing you are thankful for on a piece of paper and put it in a jar. This simple act of counting your blessings creates a well of gratitude that in turn creates a positive attitude and provides something to turn to when things get tough.

ONE SIMPLE THING: BAKE SODA BREAD

Making a loaf of bread and including it in a ritual is an excellent way to celebrate Lughnasadh. Traditionally bread was baked from newly harvested wheat and blessed in the church. Then it was broken into quarters and placed in the four corners of the barn to protect the grain over the winter. A quick, easy loaf to make is soda bread, which requires no kneading, proving or fiddling about with yeast.

WHAT YOU NEED

- 500g wholemeal flour
- 2 tsp salt
- 1 tsp bicarbonate of soda
- 400ml whole milk
- juice of a lemon

1. Preheat the oven to 180°C fan/200°C/gas 6.

2. Sift the flour, salt and bicarbonate of soda into a bowl.

3. Mix the milk and lemon juice together to make buttermilk, then pour it into a well in the centre of the flour. Mix with a fork to form a soft dough.

4. Tip the dough onto a floured surface and shape it into a circle. Put on a lightly floured baking sheet and cut a cross into the top with a sharp knife.

5. Bake for about 40 minutes. Cool on a wire rack.

A Lughnasadh ritual with your witchy crew

Cast your circle (see *Summer Solstice: The Magic Circle*). Set up your altar and place it inside the circle, facing towards the north. Place on it your ceremonial tools, a golden candle, an animal skull and a loaf of bread. Invite your friends into the circle and light the candle.

You say: "Welcome everyone. We have come here today to celebrate Lughnasadh, the first harvest, and to thank Mother Earth for the goodness that comes from the soil and the benefits it brings. From this day onwards, the sun descends into the darkness of winter. Life, growth, death and rebirth have come full circle so let us be grateful for the last summer days."

Everyone says: "We stand in this circle to thank Mother Earth for all she provides."

You hold up the loaf of bread and say: "The first harvesting season is here, that of the grain, and with it comes food for our table and hope to feed our souls. We praise the God Lugh, after whom this festival is named, and who instils the grain with his spirit."

Everyone says: "Praise to Lugh."

You pass the loaf around the circle. Everyone breaks off a piece and eats it.

You say: "We stand in this circle to thank Lugh and Mother Earth for this loaf, for the abundance they provide, and for our friendships. Sharing this loaf reminds us that we have much to be grateful for. Let us remember this moment in the months ahead and let us promise to help each other through the darker part of the year."

Everyone says: "So mote it be."

You unwind the circle. Feasting and dancing begins.

WITCHY CRAFT

MAKE A CORN DOLLY

Making harvest tokens from the hollow stems of cereal crops dates back to pre-Christian times in Europe. Stems were plaited together in abstract shapes to house the spirit of the corn that lived in the fields. These tokens or trophies (which came to be known as 'corn dollies' in the 19th century during a revival in their making) were either burned, fed to the animals or ploughed into the fields at the start of the next season to return fertility into the land.

This custom ended with the mechanization of harvesting at the start of the 20th century, but its spirit lives on. Making a simple corn dolly is a lovely crafty way to give thanks for the harvest. Include it in a ritual, place it on your altar, or use it to decorate your home. Whether or not you choose to burn your dolly at Imbolc is up to you!

WHAT YOU NEED:

- four hollow stalks of wheat. Either go out and find some along the edge of a wheat field (with permission from the farmer) or buy some online. You could also use paper straws, although this diminishes the effect.

- strong cotton or twine

- ribbon and/or flowers

Making the four-stalk compass plait

Follow these simple steps to create your dolly.

① Tie four stalks together just below the wheat ears, using a piece of strong cotton or twine. With the ears at the bottom, spread the stalks out flat into a cross.

② Bring the top stalk down, and the top stalk up.

③ Bring the right hand stalk over, and replace with the left. It should look like this.

④ Continue until you have about 8cm of stalk left unplaited. Bring the ends of the four stalks together and tie together as shown.

⑤ Holding the two ends together, spread the wheat ears out between the wheat stalks and allow to dry.

⑥ When dry, add a ribbon* or a sprig of flowers to the middle.

* Different colours of ribbon have different meanings: white for purity; brown for earth; green for germinating corn; gold for ripening wheat; orange for the sun; red for warmth; and blue for truth.

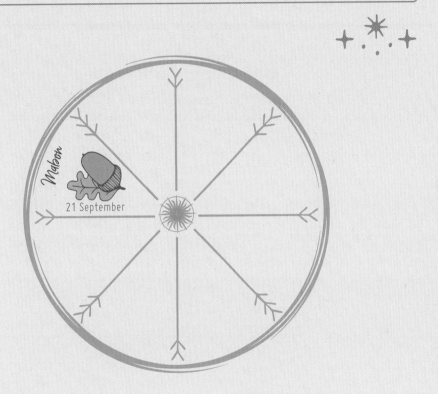

Sabbat of Mabon, the Autumn Equinox: 21 September*

Autumn equinox: The second harvest. Seeds are dispersed. A time to take responsibility for our actions.

As the days get shorter and colder, it is really tempting to stay indoors, hunker by a fire with your crystals and spells and shut the world out. But this would be a shame; you would miss the magic out there waiting for you to discover it. A walk in a park, forest, beside a river or along a coastal path will reward you with wonderful things: a conker shining in its split case; damsons dripping from a tree; elderberries about to burst; and rosehips glowing orange in the autumn sun. This is a time of rich abundance that should not be missed.

The autumn equinox* (which since 1970 has also been known as Mabon) is when celebrations take place in thanks for the second harvest. Once again, days and nights are of equal length as the Earth tilts at a right angle to the sun, shining directly over the equator. The world is in balance as the Northern and Southern Hemispheres receive the same amount of sunlight and darkness.

The autumn equinox is the second of three pagan harvest festivals (following Lughnasadh and before Samhain), when farmers congratulated themselves for a successful harvest and healthy animals or took stock if things had not gone to plan. While most of us do not have fields to mow or cattle to look after, we can use the energy of this time to reassess our lives and make plans for the darker days ahead. It is a time of rest and reflection. The world has reached equilibrium, a time of balance, and we can, too. Keep that thought in mind as you meditate or cast a spell. You are on the cusp of transition. From now on, days will be shorter and darker; make sure you are ready for them.

Traditionally, the autumn equinox was also when people gathered and partied. All that food (and drink) around was the perfect excuse to eat, dance and make merry. Gather your witchy crew together and enjoy 'cakes and ale' after your ritual. There is real magic in the simple act of eating and drinking together.

* In the Northern Hemisphere, Mabon falls on or around 21 September. If you are in the Southern Hemisphere, it will be on or around 20 March.

On your Mabon altar

There is plenty to choose from now. Heap your altar like you are at a harvest festival. You could put fruit and veg in a basket, like a cornucopia, a symbol of autumn. An apple is a must, as are any foraging finds such as sloes, rose hips, acorns and damsons. Orange and red candles feel right, but you could also use black and white to reflect the equilibrium of the season. Add a crystal or two of your choice and some leaves from a favourite tree, and you are all set.

THE MAGIC OF TREES

Any witch worth her besom should know her trees. These wise and venerable plants have much to give us and there is plenty to learn from them. The time around the autumn equinox when the leaves are falling is the ideal time to get to know trees better. As the leaves tumble, gather some up and use them for identification. Take a look at the outline of the trunk and bare branches, now revealed, for further clues. These five are magical at any time of year:

Oak

The king of the forest is synonymous with strength and steadfastness and has been venerated by different cultures for millennia. It is an important tree for Druids (the word 'druid' is often translated as 'oak knowledge' or 'oak seer'), who see it as a tree of power. Country folklore gives it healing powers: it was said that walking around its trunk would cause any ailment to be carried off by a bird. In Wales, it was thought that if you rubbed an oak with the palm of your hand on Midsummer Day, you would stay well all year. Whether or not any of that is true, sit beneath an oak and you can feel its strength and wisdom run through you. Work with it to direct and channel this energy.

How you will know it: The oak's paw-shaped leaves are easy to recognize as are its fruits, acorns, and its bark, which is gnarly with ridges and fissures.

Birch

The delicate femininity of the birch gives it its alternative names: White Lady of the Woods or Queen of the Woods. Often growing in a clearing, spotlit by sunlight, it has a fairy-like quality. Magically, it is known for its protective abilities: besoms were made from its twiggy branches and used to drive out bad spirits and to sweep the boundaries of a property to keep it safe. Maypoles and Yule logs are also made from it.

How you will know it: tall (it can grow up to 100ft) and slender, the birch has bright green leaves that turn yellow in autumn, and catkins in spring. Its bark is ghostly white with a papery texture that grows speckled with dark fissures as it ages.

Witch way: using the tip of a burned birch tip, write a promise or a wish on a piece of birch bark. Keep it safe and your wish will be fulfilled. You could also include a little birch bark or dried leaf in an incense blend and burn at the start of any important journey or new stage of your life.

OAK

Ash

Shrouded in mystical associations, the ash is a tree of enchantment and healing. In Norse mythology it is known as Yggdrasil, the World Tree, spanning many realms and associated with Odin (see *Beltane: Runes*). Ash wands are used to direct healing energy, and ash 'keys' (the name for its seeds) are thought to protect against evil. Leaves placed under a pillow will encourage prophetic dreams.

How you will know it: tall and graceful, the Ash tree can grow to heights of 50m. Its bark is pale brown/grey and it has smooth twigs with velvety buds. Its leaves move in the direction of the sun and stay green when they fall.

Yew

Incredibly, some yew trees live to be 900 years old. This longevity, and the fact that they regenerate from branches that grow into the ground to form new stems, makes them symbolic of life and death. In Irish mythology, the yew is one of the five sacred Guardian Trees brought from the otherworld by a tall stranger (the others are oak, ash, apple and hazel). Branches from the tree were used to light Beltane bonfires. (See also *Winter Plants for Remedies and Spells*).

How you will know it: you will recognize this tree immediately – the trunk is reddish-brown and the leaves are dark green and needle-like. It has bright red (poisonous) berries in autumn and the oldest ones are usually big and hollow enough to stand inside.

Hawthorn

The hawthorn has long been considered a magical tree in Ireland, where it was once believed that fairies inhabited its branches. Bad luck came to anyone who cut one down. Hawthorn's dense thorniness makes it an ideal hedging plant, but it can often be spotted growing alone, its twisted shape silhouetted against stormy skies on prehistoric barrows, hills and beside sacred wells. Thought to stand on the threshold of the otherworld, it is a tree shrouded in magic and superstition. Some people are still wary of its association with fairies and witches and will not have it in the house. Others see its May blooms as symbolic of love and festoon it around churches and include it in wedding bouquets. (See also *Beltane Plants for Remedies and Spells*).

How you will know it: The hawthorn bristles with thorns borne on a tangle of twiggy branches. It blossoms in May, when its froth of white flowers is covered with pollinating insects.

Apples: the witch's fruit

Now is apple harvest time. The delicate blossom of spring orchards has magically turned into bewitching orbs of delicious fruit. Apples feature in folk stories (Snow White was put to sleep by a poisoned apple), the Bible (Adam and Eve are thrown out of Eden after he ate one) and Arthurian legend (a wounded King Arthur was spirited away by fairy queens to Avalon, the Isle of Apples). The mysterious plant, mistletoe (see *Winter Plants for Remedies and Spells*), often grows on apple trees. But perhaps most intriguing of all, if you cut the fruit in half horizontally, a secret is revealed: the seeds are arranged in a perfect pentangle.

MAKE AUTUMN POTPOURRI

There is nothing like filling the house with evocative scents of the woodland to set the mood for a ritual or spell. One of the easiest ways to do this is to make your own potpourri, using what you can find outdoors supplemented with some fruit and spices.

1. Go for a walk and collect dry plant material like pine-cones, acorns, bark, small twigs and leaves. Take them home and leave by a radiator or in some other warm place until they are completely dry and any insects have evacuated.

2. Preheat the oven to a low temperature, i.e. 65°C. Slice an orange and a lime into 1cm-wide slices, pat dry with a cloth, then place on a metal rack above a baking tray. Put in the oven for four hours until the slices have dried out. Allow to cool.

3. Crush a couple of cinnamon sticks, a nutmeg and a few cloves in a mortar and pestle. Add a few star anise to the mix for a decorative, spicy flourish.

4. Mix everything together, keeping the proportions at roughly ten parts woodland plant material to two parts spice and fruit slices combined.

5. Transfer to a lidded jar and leave for a couple of weeks, shaking the jar once a day.

6. Pour the mixture out into a ceramic bowl and enjoy the perfumed air.

APPLE TREE

AUTUMN PLANTS FOR REMEDIES AND SPELLS

As the wheel of the year turns, the choice of plants for a witch to use in spells lessens. Annual herbs such as basil disappear but others hold on; some, like sturdy mint, are pretty good all year round. You will not have to look far to find these robust herbs to use in any potions and lotions you are concocting.

Lovage *(Levisticum officinale)*: In the Middle Ages, this leafy herb was said to have magical properties and was fed to cattle on Midsummer Day to protect them from evil witches. The medieval abbess Hildegard von Bingen thought it had healing powers and recommended it to those with respiratory problems. It was revered by the Ancient Greeks, who associated it with the Goddess Aphrodite and made it into an infusion to soothe gastric and bladder problems. More usually, however, lovage was seen as a love charm: young women put it in their shoes or bath water to attract a suitable partner. Aside from its magical potential, lovage's intense flavour, similar to celery, makes it a welcome addition to hearty food like stews and roasts.

Crab apple *(Malus sylvestris)*: Even before heritage varieties were grown, the small, thorny crab apple was found in British hedgerows and along the edges of woodland. Too hard and bitter to eat unless made into jams and jellies, it was used by our forebears in a variety of superstitious ways. The pips were thrown into the fire while saying the name of the one you loved; if the pips exploded, your love was true. In Scotland, young women put a crab apple under their pillow on St. Andrew's day, then took the apple to church; the first man they met in the porch would be their husband. The juice, known as 'verjuice', was used to treat sprains, cramp and as a laxative. Best of all, unicorns were believed to live under crab apple trees. Nowadays the crab apple's most useful function is as pollinator for other apple trees. Bees love its blossom and cannot leave it alone.

Hazel *(Corylus avellana)*: In Celtic legend, nine magic hazel trees grew over the Well of Wisdom, dropping their nuts into its water. These nuts created bubbles of mystical inspiration and had prophetic powers. Maybe this is the reason that hazel sticks are so often used for wands and to dowse for water. The Anglo Saxon word *haesl* means 'baton of authority'. There is also an ancient connection between hazel and matters of the heart and fertility. In Devon, there was a tradition of giving a new bride a switch of hazel to boost her chances of pregnancy. Cattle was also driven through a Beltane bonfire with a whip made from hazel to protect them against disease and bad things in general.

Mint (*Mentha*): The cleansing and healing properties of mint are well known. The strength and clarity of its fragrance goes straight to the olfactory system, bringing with it all manner of benefits, from an invigorating mouth wash to a headache easer and digestive aid. It also features prominently in rituals and spells, especially those to attract cash, lure love and boost divinatory powers. Try making mint tea before reading the tarot, runes or scrying. Easy to recognize and grow, it should be a staple of any witch's herbarium. Best plant it in a pot, however: it can romp away and bully other plants out of the border.

Witch ways: Here are some ways to make the most of this season's plants. See *A Witch's Herbal* for directions on drying herbs.

- Make a wand from a slim hazel branch. Its forked branches can be used as dowsing rods for divination.

- Make jelly from foraged crab apples and serve it as part of your autumn equinox celebrations.

- To attract love, make a pouch from red fabric and fill it with dried lovage, rose petals, juniper berries and a piece of paper stating your desire.

- Put a few mint leaves in the bag where you keep your tarot cards, runes or black mirror. The leaves' cleansing properties will keep the energy clear and fresh.

MINT

CRYSTALS FOR MABON

You may have favourite crystals that you know well and always work with, and these are good at any time of the year. Sometimes, though, it is good to try something new. At this time of transformation, when the light is fading and we prepare for the dark months, refresh the magic by working with a new stone. These feel powerful now:

White opal: the seductive, opalescent 'eye stone'.
This gem has long been associated with magic and luck. Lustrous and mysterious, it has a uniquely milky opalescence that flashes different colours with the slightest movement, as though something is flickering inside. The Ancient Greeks were so dazzled by opal that they thought it gave them the power of prophecy and would protect them from disease. A seductive stone, opal releases inhibitions and can be used to ignite passion and desire. It can also settle and calm a restless mind.

Malachite: pure nature in crystal form.
Rich green, dense and opaque, sometimes shot through with bands of various shades of green agate, malachite is like a crystallized piece of pure nature. It comes from just below the earth's surface, forming at shallow depths as stalactites, and was first found in Egypt and Israel over 4,000 years ago. It has always been credited with powers of transformation and healing. Egyptian pharaohs lined the inside of their head dresses with it to amplify wisdom and crushed it into powder for eyeshadow. Eye-shaped bands or 'eye stones' can be found in some pieces, and it is thought to stimulate clear vision and insight: some witches use it for scrying.

Aquamarine: mystical jewel of visionaries and mermaids.
This cool, pale-blue stone was thought to be mermaid treasure. You can see why: it is a mystical, sparkling jewel of visionary powers. Its colour and translucency have always linked it to the sea: Roman sailors called it 'water of the sea' and carried it to protect them from misfortune. Blue is also the colour of the skies and heaven, and aquamarine has always been valued by prophets, shaman, and mystics. It is the stone to call on in times of stress. Working with it calms frayed nerves.

Hematite: the grounding stone of Mars.
The Ancient Greeks associated hematite with Mars, god of War, which is spookily prescient of them as it one of the most abundant minerals found on that planet's surface. There is also plenty of it to be found on Earth: it lies just below the surface and is the most important ore of iron. Varying in colour from earthy red to charcoal black, it has a shimmering metallic lustre that brightens further when polished. Hematite has a weighty presence that feels anchoring and steady. Meditate with a piece cupped in both hands to ground yourself and connect with the Earth, especially if a big life change has shaken your world.

MEDITATING WITH CRYSTALS

Although all you need to meditate is a quiet spot and a (reasonably) still mind, crystals can help you focus and bring clarity to your practice.

After you have switched off your phone and found a peaceful place to sit, choose your crystal. You can do this by instinct, choose one that has a particular purpose or use one that chimes with the wheel of the year. A clear crystal like citrine or another quartz is thought to help clear the mind, for example.

Hold the crystal and see how it feels. Communicate with it, either in your thoughts or aloud – you could express what you hope to gain from the meditation, if anything – and thank it for its help. Place it beside you or in your lap and be aware of its presence. Become aware of your breath, counting each inhale and exhale or just letting it flow. Then see where your mind and the crystal takes you.

MABON TRADITIONS AND CUSTOMS

Unlike the spring equinox, a joyful time of growth and light, the autumn equinox has a more melancholic air as things come to their natural end and darkness falls. It is a time of transition, leaving the warmth of summer behind as the world prepares for winter.

Michaelmas and Goose Day

The Catholic feast day honouring St. Michael, known as Michaelmas, takes place on 29 September. St. Michael fought off Satan and his evil angels, replacing darkness with light. The saint was seen as a protector during the winter months.

Traditionally, Michaelmas marked the end of the harvest season; farm labourers were paid for their work, rent was due and new contracts were made. A fattened goose fed on the stubble from the fields was eaten to ensure prosperity in the year ahead. As an old rhyme stated:

Eat a goose on Michaelmas Day
Want not for money all the year

Goose fairs were held to buy and sell geese for the table.

Watching the sun come up

Getting up early to watch the sunrise is a powerful act at any time of year, but even more so at an equinox. Druids gather at stone circles at Mabon, as they do at Ostara and at the summer solstice, to watch the sun come up, to thank it for the harvest and to prepare for the imminent darkness of winter.

Around the world, similar practices are taking place. People cluster on top of the Bronze Age observatory in Kokino, near the town of Kumanovo, North Macedonia, to observe the rising of the sun. The same thing happens at Chaco Canyon, another ancient observatory in New Mexico, USA. Whereas in China and Vietnam, it is the moon that is centre stage: the Moon (or mid-Autumn) Festival, takes place when the full moon is nearest to the equinox. Mooncakes are eaten in the moonlight.

Dandelion and burdock

During the Middle Ages, dandelion and burdock, a drink made from fermented dandelion and the burdock root, was drunk at this time of year. This peculiar potion was thought to cleanse the blood and prepare the body for the winter days ahead. Out of favour for a long time, dandelion and burdock is now produced commercially as a carbonated drink. One for your autumn equinox feast, perhaps.

MABON RITUALS AND SPELLS

As the wheel turns towards winter and sunny days become increasingly scarce, it can be tempting to retreat and wait for the return of the sun. Adopt a positive approach instead: be thankful for the harvest and the summer with simple rituals and spells, and ask for guidance to help you through the dark months.

A simple solo ritual

As the leaves fall from the trees and plants die back into the soil, a cheering and positive thing to do is plan for spring. One way to do this is to plant bulbs. Now is the time to get them in the earth so they can put their roots down and flower next spring. You do not need a big garden to do this, a few bulbs in a pot will deliver plenty of pleasure.

Use the time you spend planting them as an opportunity to think about what other things you want to grow next year. This could be your career, a new relationship, your witchy practice or something else altogether. With each bulb you put in the ground, visualize these things establishing and flourishing.

Witch way: Here are some spooky bulbs to try now.

- Narcissus 'Little Witch': a pretty little yellow daffodil.
- Hyacinth 'Midnight Mystery': a black hyacinth with a heavenly scent.
- Tulip 'Queen of the Night': a gorgeous deep purple tulip.

A SIMPLE WISH

For this wish-making ritual, you will need some fabric and a little patience.

Cut a piece of fabric into one or several strips that are around 20cm long and 5cm wide. Hold a strip in both hands and charge it with a wish or healing energy for yourself or those close to you. Tie the cloth to the branch of an apple tree, preferably one that will not be disturbed. If you or a friend has one in your garden, that would be perfect. Now wait. As the cloth disintegrates, your wish will be answered.

A Mabon ritual with your witchy crew

Cast your circle (see *Summer Solstice: The Magic Circle*). Set up your altar and face it to the north. Place on it your ceremonial tools, a gold candle, pine cones, autumn leaves, an apple sliced in half, a sharp knife and a jug of apple juice or cider and some glasses. Invite your friends into the circle and light the candle.

You say: "Welcome everyone. We have come here today to celebrate the autumn equinox – the second harvest. The wheel of the year has turned and we are entering the dark months. As we pick fruit and enjoy the harvest, we also prepare for the winter, a time of quiet reflection."

Hold the apple up and display its two halves to everyone.

You say: "The apple is a symbol of wisdom and the divine. Let it guide us through these dark months. It has five points at its heart, secretly enclosed within a sacred pentacle. Each point represents a different element. One is for earth, one is for air, one is for fire and one is for water. The final point is for spirit."

Everyone says: "We respect the apple and what it represents."

You say: "Let us make the most of the sacred festival of the autumn equinox and use this ritual to deepen our wisdom."

Take the knife and cut the apple into slices. Pass the slices and the glasses of apple juice around the circle.

You say: "As we eat the fruit of the apple tree and drink its juice, we call upon its spirit to help us become wiser. Let us take some time to think how we can increase our knowledge and understanding of ourselves, others and the world around us."

Everyone is silent as they eat the apple, drink the juice, and think.

You say: "We deepen our intention to grow in wisdom and knowledge. So mote it be."

Everyone says: "So mote it be."

You close the circle. Feasting and dancing begins.

WITCHY CRAFT

MAKE AN APPLE WAND

A wand has a number of magical purposes: it can be used to point and direct energy during a ritual, to consecrate a sacred space or to draw a magic circle. An athame, the witch's double-edged dagger (see *What a Witch Needs*) can also be used for these.

This wand is made from apple wood because apples are all around us at this time of year and it is a particularly witchy fruit tree. However, you may feel that another tree suits you better. You could choose oak if you want your wand to have power and strength, for example, or ash for its powers of prophecy and divination.

WHAT YOU NEED

- a straight piece of wood
- a sharp knife
- sandpaper
- linseed or teak oil (optional)
- a thin piece of leather or some strong string or twine
- feathers, crystals and beads, to decorate

Making the wand

Follow these simple steps to create your wand.

①

Find a piece of wood in an orchard or where apples grow in the wild. Do not cut it from the tree; look on the ground where it has fallen. The right piece of wood will manifest – it should be as straight as possible and not too heavy. Thank the tree for the gift of the branch and leave an offering such as some apple juice or spring water (nothing polluting!)

②

Remove the bark with the knife and nip off any irregularities, bits of branches and so on.

③

With the knife, shape the wood so that it tapers at one end.

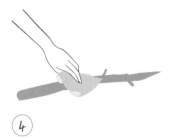

4

Sand it with sandpaper until it is smooth. You could brush it with a light coat of linseed or teak oil to protect it, but this is not essential.

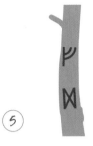

5

Decorate it by writing or carving symbols or runes into it. These should be carefully chosen and have particular meaning to you. (See *Beltane: Runes and the Tarot*.)

6

Drill a hole in one end to thread a length of string or a piece of leather through to carry it.

7

Some witches add a crystal to its narrowest end, or feathers. How you personalize it is up to you.

8

Consecrate your wand as you would other magical tools (see *Beltane: Runes and the Tarot* for more on consecrating your tools).

9

Optional: designate your apple wand to a particular goddess or god. Hold it above your head, gather other witches around, chant the name of the deity and channel them. Then you can use the wand to invoke them in rituals.

ABOUT THE AUTHOR

Clare Gogerty

Clare lives on a smallholding in rural Herefordshire, which she intends to open as a spiritual retreat. The sound of shamanic drumming often comes from her orchard where she has built a stone labyrinth, and herbal remedies are frequently cooked up in the kitchen. She has been interested in magic, folklore and Druidry since childhood, and is often on an adventure to find standing stones or an ancient path. Find her on Instagram: @waysidewitch

A former magazine editor, Clare is now a freelance journalist and author, writing about spirituality and travel for various magazines and newspapers. In 2019, her book *Beyond the Footpath: mindful adventures for modern pilgrims* was published, followed by *Sacred Places: where to find wonder in the world* in 2020.

Acknowledgements

Thank you to my father John Gogerty, master of the pendulum, who introduced me to many of the subjects in this book.

Also, gratitude to all the witches, hedge witches, druids and shamans keeping the old ways alive and who know that magic is all around us if we know where to look.

And respect and appreciation to the clever team at David and Charles, especially Ame Verso whose idea this was, Jessica Cropper and Samantha Staddon. A big thank you also goes to my project editor Claire Coakley. Thank you all for your professionalism and support.

INDEX

Names of manufacturers and product ranges are
provided for the information of readers, with no
intention to infringe copyright or trademarks.

A catalogue record for this book is available from
the British Library.

ISBN-13: 9781446308806 paperback
ISBN-13: 9781446380901 EPUB
ISBN-13: 9781446380895 PDF

This book has been printed on paper from approved
suppliers and made from pulp from sustainable sources.

Printed in China through Asia Pacific Offset for:
David and Charles, Ltd
Suite A, Tourism House, Pynes Hill, Exeter, EX2 5WS

10 9 8 7 6 5 4

Publishing Director: Ame Verso
Editor: Jessica Cropper
Project Editor: Claire Coakley
Head of Design: Sam Staddon
Design & Illustration: Emma Teagle
Pre-press Designer: Ali Stark
Production Manager: Beverley Richardson

David and Charles publishes high-quality books on a
wide range of subjects. For more information visit
www.davidandcharles.com.

Layout of the digital edition of this book may vary
depending on reader hardware and display settings.